Priapea: Songs for a Phallic God

An Intermediate Latin Reader

Latin Text with Running Vocabulary and Commentary

Tyler Gau
Evan Hayes
Stephen Nimis

Priapea: Songs for a Phallic God: An Intermediate Latin Reader
Latin Text with Running Vocabulary and Commentary

First Edition

© 2017 by Tyler Gau, Evan Hayes, and Stephen Nimis

All rights reserved. Subject to the exception immediately following, this book may not be reproduced, in whole or in part, in any form (beyond copying permitted by Sections 107 and 108 of the U.S. Copyright Law and except by reviewers for the public press), without written permission from the publisher. The authors have made a version of this work available (via email) under a Creative Commons Attribution-Noncommercial-Share Alike 3.0 License. The terms of the license can be accessed at www.creativecommons.org.

Accordingly, you are free to copy, alter and distribute this work under the following conditions:

> 1. You must attribute the work to the author (but not in a way that suggests that the author endorses your alterations to the work).
>
> 2. You may not use this work for commercial purposes.
>
> 3. If you alter, transform or build up this work, you may distribute the resulting work only under the same or similar license as this one.

ISBN-10: 1940997836

ISBN-13: 9781940997834

Published by Faenum Publishing, Ltd.

Cover Design: Evan Hayes

Fonts: Garamond

editor@faenumpublishing.com

Table of Contents

Acknowledgements v

Introduction ix

Glossing Conventions xvii

Abbreviations Used in the Commentary xix

Grammatical Terms Used in the Commentary xxi

    Uses of Cases xx

    Uses of the Subjunctive xxv

    Indirect Statements, Questions and Commands xxvii

    Conditional Sentences xxviii

    Rhetorical Terms xxix

    Other Terminology xxx

Priapea: Text and Commentary 1

Glossary 75

Acknowledgments

The idea for this project grew out of work that we, the authors, did with support from Miami University's Undergraduate Summer Scholars Program, for which we thank Martha Weber and the Office of Advanced Research and Scholarship. Work on the series, of which this volume is a part, was generously funded by the Joanna Jackson Goldman Memorial Prize through the Honors Program at Miami University. We owe a great deal to Carolyn Haynes and the 2010 Honors & Scholars Program Advisory Committee for their interest and confidence in the project.

The technical aspects of the project were made possible through the invaluable advice and support of Bill Hayes, Christopher Kuo, and Daniel Meyers. The equipment and staff of Miami University's Interactive Language Resource Center were a great help along the way. We are also indebted to the Perseus Project, especially Gregory Crane and Bridget Almas, for their technical help and resources. We also profited greatly from advice and help on the POD process from Geoffrey Steadman. All responsibility for errors, however, rests with the authors themselves.

Cui dono lepidum novum libellum
arida modo pumice expolitum?
mi mater, tibi: namque tu solebas
meas esse aliquid putare nugas.

Introduction

The aim of this book is to make the *Priapea* (or *Corpus Priapeorum* or *Carmina Priapea*) accessible to intermediate students of Ancient Latin. The running vocabulary and grammatical commentary are meant to provide everything necessary to read each page so that readers can progress through the text, improving their knowledge of Latin while enjoying a fascinating group of poems.

The *Priapea* is a great text for intermediate readers. The sentence structure is fairly simple, and the range of syntax is rather narrow. However, there are many off-color jokes and double entendre that require some thoughtful attention to the connotations of many ordinary words. There is considerable wittiness deployed in creating variations on a small number of obscene themes and scenarios, so that there are examples of the whole range of technique in Roman poetic practice. The poems are centered around the rustic and ithyphallic god Priapus. This god, whose name gives us the Engish word "priapism," the condition of having a lasting and painful erection, is a minor god with very little mythology. He is usually represented as a wooden statue with an oversized and erect penis, which he threatens to use on anyone who is caught stealing from his garden. Indeed, the largest group of poems in the collection are warnings to thieves whom Priapus threatens to penetrate in one of three orifices, depending on the status of the offender. Other poems make fun of Priapus or represent him begging for favors or receiving dedications. Another group of poems, often shocking in detail, rails against older and undesirable women, whose sexual appetites are portrayed as vile and disgusting. The humor is strongly weighted toward men and their "weapons," in this way reflecting the pleasure Romans took in performing their masculinity in various contexts. The classic discussion of these topics is Amy Richilin's *The Gardens of Priapus: Sexuality and Aggression in Roman Humor.*

Greek and Latin *Priapea*

Priapus is a rustic god whose origin seems to be in Asia minor—Lampsacus is identified as his birth place in several poems. A number of examples survive in the *Greek Anthology* which are similar to the Latin poems in this volume. Many of these are dedications from people in various walks of life, sometimes with requests from the god for fertility or potency, or for relief from the pangs of love. Several are from sailors seeking a safe voyage. The Latin *Priapea* are more narrowly focussed on the rustic god and his garden. Besides the 80 of this collection, Priapic poems appear in the works of other poets, like Catullus, Horace, and Martial, indicating the popularity of the kind of humor found here. Priapus is also the "angry god" in Petronius' *Satyricon*, who causes the hero Encolpius so many troubles in his wanderings, a comic analogue to the role of Poseidon in the *Odyssey* and Juno in the *Aeneid*.

Date and Authorship of the *Priapea*

The manuscript tradition ascribes the *Priapea* to Vergil, which shocked Renaissance scholars for whom these poems seemed unworthy of the great Augustan poet. The theory for several centuries was that poems by multiple authors had been collected by someone and attached to the genuine poems of Vergil. In the twentieth century the weight of scholarly opinion has shifted back to a single author, but not to Vergil. Instead, Ovid or Martial has been suggested as the author of the whole collection, based on examples of similar diction in those authors, but this could just be evidence that those authors were familiar with the collection. Even so, most scholars emphasize the continuities among the poems rather than their heterogeneity. Most recently, O'Connor has argued that a skillful editor collected the poems and perhaps wrote some of them himself. The poems are thought to date either to the Augustan age (27 BCE–14 CE) or to the time of Martial (died. c. 102 CE), but this too is uncertain. What is certain is that there was a continuous tradition of such Priapic poetry that included the *Priapea* and examples from several other poets. The collection is certainly a miscellany in some respects, but there is also evidence of an overall shaping of the material that suggests a single author or editor.

The Content of the Poems

Most of the poems fall into a small number of groups. The largest group contains threats by Priapus to use his formidable member against thieves. These include 6, 11, 13, 15, 17, 22, 23, 24, 25, 28, 30, 31, 35, 44, 51, 52, 56, 58, 59, 67, 69, 71, 72, 77.

Other poems highlight the divine status of Priapus and compare him and his accouterments with other gods and goddesses (9, 20, 36, 39, 53, 75), while others emphasize his humble wooden origins or complain about his treatment at the hands of others (10, 26, 33, 55, 73, 76, 77).

Some are based on dedications to Priapus of various kinds, whether of verses or fruits (4, 16, 21, 27, 34, 37, 40, 41, 42, 47, 50, 60, 61, 63, 70). These frequently sound the *do ut des* (I give in order to get) theme.

Some deprecate older women (12, 32, 46, 57) or warn chaste women to stay away (8, 10, 66).

In the first two and last two poems of the collection, the poet himself addresses the reader or Priapus (1, 2, 79, 80).

The Meters of the Poems

The poems are in three different meters: elegaic couplets, hendecasyllables and choliambs. Elegaic couplets are used in a wide variety of contexts by Catullus, Propertius, Ovid, Tibullus and others. Hendecasyllables are used frequently by Catullus, but they also are the main element of Sapphic meter. Choliambs ("limping iambs") are used most frequently in invective. All of these meters have Greek precedents. They are distributed as follows:

Hendecasyllables: 2, 4, 6, 8, 10, 12, 14, 17, 19, 23, 25, 26, 28, 29, 32, 34, 35, 37, 41, 45, 46, 48, 50, 52, 56, 57, 59, 61, 64, 66, 69, 70, 75, 76, 77.

Elegaic couplets: 1, 3, 5, 7, 9, 11, 13, 15, 16, 18, 20, 21, 22, 24, 27, 30, 33, 38, 40, 42, 43, 49, 53, 54, 55, 60, 62, 65, 67, 68, 71, 72, 73, 74, 80.

Choliambs: 31, 36, 47, 51, 58, 63, 78, 79.

Here is the scheme for each of these three meters, where "×" indicates an anceps syllable:

Hendecasyllables: $- - - \cup \cup - \cup - \cup - -$

Elegaic Couples: $- \cup \cup - \cup \cup - \| \cup \cup - \cup \cup - \cup \cup - \times$
$- \cup \cup - \cup \cup - \| - \cup \cup - \cup \cup \times$

Choliambs: $\times - \cup - \mid \times - \cup - \mid \cup - - -$

Comparison with canonical poets who use these meters indicates a high level of craftsmanship in the *Priapea* that is inconsistent with the idea of a miscellany of multiple authors. Indeed, as Parker notes, one of the striking things about these poems is the stark contrast between their low subject matter and the perfection of their artistry (44). Our author shows stricter regularity in many cases, such as the spondee opening of the hendecasyllable line, where Catullus frequently substitutes a trochee or iamb.

Latin Sexual Vocabulary

Latin has a broad range of polite and impolite ways of speaking of sex. The *Priapea* specialize in the latter, but show a sophisticated humor as well. A full treatment of the subject is J. N. Adams, *The Latin Sexual Vocabulary* (Duckworth, London, 1982). The following general remarks, meant to help the reader navigate the *Priapea*, are based on his work.

1. *Mentula* and its synonyms

Mentula is the basic obscene word for the male member. Like various English parallels, such as "dick" and "prick," it can be used generally as an insult as well. **Verpa** is a synonym that is also offensive and is also used frequently as an insult. **Penis** is much less obscene. Beyond these words, there is a vast number of metaphorical terms usually connected with shape or function, especially weapons or objects that are used to pierce something.

These include **telum** ("weapon"), **columna** ("column"), **contus** ("pole"), **sceptrum** ("sceptre"), **ventris arma** ("weapon of the belly"), **hasta** ("spear"), **pyramis** ("pyramid"), **bracchia macra** ("narrow arm"), **falx** ("sickle"), **temo** ("beam"), **capulus** ("handle"), **fascinum** ("amulet"), **nasus** ("nose").

Another common metaphor pertains to objects that are taut (**tensus**): **nervum** ("string of the bow"), **cithara** ("lyre string"), **vena** ("blood vessel").

Sexual parts can be addressed or rebuked as though they were persons or animals. A *mentula* can be said to have a "head" or an "eye." It can be likened to a snake (**anguis**).

Coleus ("a leather sack") is a coarse word for the scrotum and is used in the plural to mean "testicles." **Vas** ("implement") is similarly used in the plural for testicles.

2. Designations of the female genitalia

Cunnus is the common obscene word for the female pudenda, equivalent in force to the English word "cunt." It originally meant a ditch, and **fossa** is also used to designate the same thing. The word **hiatus** ("gap") is a vulgar word for a worn-out vagina or one that has been "loosened" (**laxus**) by sexual activity.

Landica is the normal word for clitoris, but because of its shape and association with the penis, it can be referred to as a **nasus** ("nose").

3. *Culus* and its synonyms

Culus is the normal obscene word for anus. Rarely it is designated by words for a meadow or garden (**pratum, hortus**). **Podex** (perhaps from *pedo*, "to fart") is used once for the buttocks. So also **clunis** and **lumbus**. Given that sex (and sexual assault) was conceived of primarily in terms of penetration, *culus* and *cunnus* often have interchangeable metaphors.

4. The vocabulary relating to sexual acts

Futuo is the most important coarse verb for penetration of the vagina and has the same insulting connotations as the English word "fuck." It can sometimes refer to anal penetration as well. It is used only of the male action: women (and boys) can only "be fucked."

Pedico is a Greek loan word referring to anal sex, whether with a male or female. **Pedicator** and **pedicatio** are derivative nouns.

Irrumo is to "put into the mouth" and thus refers to the male action of penetrating the mouth. **Irrumator** and **irrumatio** are derivative nouns. **Fellatio** refers to the act of sucking, with **fellator** as a derivative noun.

Pedicare and *irrumare* can indicate an assertion of mastery or a threat of punishment to one's enemies, as in Catullus 16: *pedicabo ego vos et irrumabo*.

Other violent verbs can be used as well, such as **scindo** ("to cut or tear"), **fodio** ("to dig"), **caedo** ("to cut"), **percido** ("to smash"), **perforo** ("to bore through"), **tero** ("to rub away").

Texts, Translations and Commentaries

Callebat, Louis. *Priapées. Collection des universités de France. Série latine 402.* Paris: Les Belles Lettres, 2012.

Codoñer, Carmen and Jun A. González Iglesias. *Priapea: Exemplaria Classica, Anejo III 2014.* Huelva: Universidad de Huelva, 2015.

Goldberg, Christiane. *Carmina Priapea: Einleitung, Interpretationen und Kommentar.* Heidelberg: Carl Winter, 1992.

Hooper, Richard, tr. *The Priapus Poems: Erotic Epigrams from Ancient Rome.* Urbana: University of Illinois Press, 1999.

Parker, W. H. *Priapea: Poems for a Phallic God.* London and Sydney: Croom Helm, 1988.

Literary Studies

Adams, J. N. *The Latin Sexual Vocabulary.* Baltimore: Johns Hopkins University Press, 1982.

Holzberg, Niklas. "Impotence? It Happened to the Best of Them! A Linear Reading of the *Corpus Priapeorum*" *Hermes*, 133 (2005), pp. 368-381.

O'Connor, Eugene M. *Symbolum Salicitatis: A study of the God Priapus as a Literary Charcter.* New York: Peter Lang, 1989.

Rankin H. D. "Petronius, Priapus and *Priapeum* LXVIII." *C&M* 27 (1966), 225-242.

Richilin, Amy. *The Garden of Priapus: Sexuality and Agresssion in Roman Humor.* New York: Oxford University Press, (rev.)1992.

Stewart, Peter. "Fine art and Coarse Art: The Image of Roman Priapus." *Art History* 20, No. 4 (1997), 475-88.

Travillian, Tyler T. *Social and Literary-Historical Studies on the Corpus Priapeorum.* Dissertation: Boston Univerity, 2011.

Uden, James. "The Vanishing Gardens of Priapus." *HSPh* 105 (2010), 189-219.

Young, Elizabeth. "*Dicere Latine*: The Art of Speaking Crudely in the *Carmina Priapea*." in *Ancient Obscenities*, ed. D. Dutsch and A. Suter (Ann Arbor: University of Michigan Press, 2015), 255-80.

How to use this book

The page-by-page vocabularies gloss all but the most common words. We have endeavored to make these glossaries as useful as possible without becoming fulsome. Words occurring frequently in the text and not glossed, or not glossed in every case, can be found in an appendix in the back, but it is our hope that most readers will not need to use this appendix often. Only minimal information is given in the page by page glossaries, for which see "Glossing Conventions" below.

The commentary is almost exclusively grammatical, explaining subordinate clauses, case uses and idioms. A brief grammatical appendix details the meaning of the technical terms used in the commentary, although most of these will be familiar to intermediate readers of Latin. A good strategy is to read a passage in Latin, check the glossary for unusual words and consult the commentary as a last resort.

The literary commentaries cited in the bibliography above contain extensive information and discussion of all aspects of the text, with copious bibliography. Our contribution has a more limited focus aimed at intermediate readers, but we have made full use of these and other resources.

The Latin text is based on Baehrens, *Poetae Latini Minores* (Leipzig 1879, pp. 58-87). It was digitized by Harm-Jan van Dam of Leiden and is posted on the Latin Library. Here and there we have corrected some errors and made minor changes in the name of readability, sometimes accepting suggestions from later editions. This is not a scholarly edition; for that one should turn to the editions cited above.

An Important Disclaimer:

This volume is a self-published "Print on Demand" (POD) book, and it has not been vetted or edited in the usual way by publishing professionals. There are sure to be some factual and typographical errors in the text, for which we apologize in advance. The volume is also available only through online distributors, since each book is printed when ordered online. However, this publishing channel and format also account for the low price of the book; and it is a simple matter to make changes when they come to our attention. For this reason, any corrections or suggestions for improvement are welcome and will be addressed as quickly as possible in future versions of the text.

Please e-mail corrections or suggestions to editor@faenumpublishing.com.

About the Authors:

Tyler Gau is a 2013 graduate in Classics at Miami University.

Evan Hayes is a graduate in Classics and Philosophy at Miami University and the 2011 Joanna Jackson Goldman Scholar.

Stephen Nimis is an Emeritus Professor of Classics at Miami University and Professor of English and Comparative Literature at the American University in Cairo.

Glossing Conventions

Adjectives of two and three terminations will be formatted thus:

bonus, -a, -um

facilis, -e

Single termination adjectives will have the genitive indicated thus:

sallax, salacis (*gen.*)

Participles will generally be glossed as a verb, but some participles (particularly where their verbal force has been weakened) are glossed as adjectives: e.g.

decens, decentis (*gen.*): appropriate; **valens, valentis** (*gen.*): strong

barbatus, -a, -um: bearded; **remotus, -a, -um**: remote

Adverbs will be identified as such (adv.) when there is some ambiguity.

Regular infinitives are indicated by conjugation number: e.g.,

laudo (1) to praise

moneo (2) to warn

Where principal parts are predictable, as in the case of most first conjugation verbs, only the conjugation number will be given in the glossary. This format is used even in the case of unpredictable perfect forms, if the word occurring in the text is based on the present stem (present, future, imperfect tenses). Elsewhere the principal parts will be provided in their standard form.

Simple syntactical information such as "+ *gen.*" or "+ *inf.*" will often be cited in the glossary with verbs and adjectives. However, the lexical information given for most words is minimal and sometimes specific to the context. To get a broader sense of the peculiarities of language in the *Priapea*, it will be necessary to consult the commentaries or critical literature cited above.

Abbreviations used in the commentary

abl. – ablative
abs. – absolute
acc. – accusative
act. – active
adj. – adjective
adv. – adverb
apoc. – apocopated
appos. – apposition
attend. – attendant
circum. – circumstantial
com. – command
comp. – comparative
concess. – concessive
dat. – dative
delib. – deliberative
desc. – description
dir. – direct
f. – feminine
fut. – future
gen. – genitive
imper. – imperative
impf. – imperfect
ind. – indirect
inf. – infinitive

intrans. – intransitive
loc. – locative
m. – masculine
neut. – neuter
neg. – negative
nom. – nominative
obj. – object
part. – participle
pass. – passive
perf. – perfect
pl. – plural
plupf. – pluperfect
pres. – present
pred. – predicate
pron. – pronoun
purp. – purpose
quest. – question
resp. – respect
s. – singular
sc. – scilicet
sep. – separation
st. – statement
subj. – subjunctive
sync. – syncopated

Grammatical Terms used in the Commentary

The grammatical terms used in the commentary are organized below according to syntactical category with brief explanations and examples. For more detailed information, see Allen and Greenough, *New Latin Grammar* (available on Perseus) or Charles Bennett *New Latin Grammar* (available on the Latin Library).

1. Uses of Cases

NOMINATIVE

The nominative case is the used for the subject of finite verbs and the predicate of verbs of being, seeming, etc.

GENITIVE

The genitive is commonly used to express a relationship between one noun and another, especially a limiting relationship. Some verbs also take the genitive as their object instead of the accusative.

Material: The genitive denotes what a thing consists of:

nigri fornicis favilla, "the ash *of a black whorehouse*"

Objective: the genitive can indicate the object of an action implied by a substantive:

curam habere loci, "to have the care *of the place*"

Partitive (genitive of the whole): The genitive indicates the whole to which a part belongs:

quicunque vestrum, "whoever *of you*"

Possession: The genitive denotes possession, including the belonging of an object, quality, feeling, or action to a person or thing:

Herculis invicti dextera, "the right hand *of unconquered Hercules*"

Predicative: A genitive can be used with verbs of being, seeming, etc.

sciscitari… unde natalium: "to question whence was *his parentage*"

Quality (characteristic, description): The genitive is used to describe a person or thing:

> *fatui* puella *cunni*, "a girl *with a foolish cunt*"

Separation: The genitive can express separation:

> libamine *mentulae* comeso, "the offering *from my prick* having been eaten"

Price or value: The genitive expresses price or value.

> non *assis* faciunt: "they do it not *for even a penny*"

After verbs and adjectives: The genitive is used to complete the meaning of certain adjectives, such as *plenus* (full of) or *egenus* (in need of). It is also used after certain verbs, such as *memini* (to remember), *misereror* (to pity), *paeniteo* (to regret), *metuo* (to fear), etc. These will be indicated in the commentary simply as "gen. after *memini*"

DATIVE

The Dative case is chiefly used to indicate the person for whom an action happens or a quality exists.

Agent: the dative expresses the agent of an action with passive verbs, especially the gerundive.

> *mihi* mentula est vocanda, "the prick must be named *by me*"

Indirect Object: The recipient of the action of the verb is put in the dative case.

> istud *caelitibus* datur *severis*, "this is given *to the severe gods*"

Possession: The dative is used to express possession with the verb esse.

> blaesa lingua *mihi* est, "*my* tongue is mispronouncing"

Predicate: the dative can be uses as the predicate of the verb esse:

> sed potuit *damno* nobis esse, "it could be our *ruin*"

Reference (advantage, interest): the dative identifies the person interested, concerned, benefited by an action.

> Cum sacrum fieret *deo salaci*, "when a sacrifice happens *for the salacious god*"

Verbs and Compound Verbs: Verbs such as *noceo* (to harm), *suadere* (persuade), etc., take the dative case, as do many verbs with a prefix, such as *impono* (to place on), *accedo* (to add to), etc.

ACCUSATIVE

The accusative case is used for the direct object of transitive verbs, for the subject of an infinitive in indirect statement and other complements of a verb, to indicate place to which, and duration of time.

Adverbial: the accusative of adjectives can be used adverbially:

> *clunem <u>excitatius altiusque</u> motat*, "she moves her buttocks *more excitedly and higher*"

Direct Object: the direct object of verbs is in the accusative case:

> *<u>qualia</u> tulisse*, "to have carried *such fruits*"

Exclamation: The accusative is used in short exclamatory phrases.

> *me miserum*, "O miserable me!"

Place to Which: Used to convey the location travelled to, often with a preposition:

> *<u>locum</u> venitis*, "you come *to a place*"

Predicative: Causative verbs like *facere* can take a second predicative accusative.

> *rivalem <u>languidum</u> reddat*, "may he make his rival *languid*"

Respect: The accusative may be used with an adjective or verb to denote the part concerned.

> *<u>frontem</u> vides cornutos*, "you see them horned *with respect to the forehead*"

Subject of Infinitives: In indirect discourse and other expressions that are complemented by an infinitive, the subject of the infinitive is in the accusative case.

> *num pudet <u>Phoebum</u> portare sagittas*, "is it not fitting that *Phoebus* carry arrows?"

Supine: Accusative supines occur after verbs of motion in order to express purpose.

> *venire credo <u>furatum</u>*, "I believe you come *in order to steal*"

ABLATIVE

Nouns in the ablative case are used often adverbially, generally expressing motion away from something, instrument, location, and many other relations.

Ablative Absolute: Combined with a participle, adjective, or noun, the ablative conveys the circumstance (time, cause, or condition) of a particular action.

    teste te: "with you as a witness"

Agent: The agent of a passive verb is expressed by the ablative usually with the preposition *ab*.

    raptus <u>ab alite sacra</u>, "snatched *by the holy eagle*"

Cause: Cause may be expressed by an ablative with or without a prespostion.

    <u>qua</u> suspicer <u>causa</u>, "*for what reason* would I suspect?"

Circumstance: a circumstance or situation attendant to a verb can be expressed with the ablative:

    stamus <u>coleis apertis</u>, "we stand *with open buttocks*"

Comparison: Comparative adjectives followed by the ablative express comparison.

    serior Hectoris <u>parente</u>, "older *than the mother* of Hector"

Degree of Difference (measure of difference) is indicated by the ablative:

    simplicius <u>multo</u> est, "it is easier *by much*"

Manner: Often with *cum*, manner is also denoted by the simple ablative.

    crisabit <u>fluctuante lumbo</u>, "she will move *with undulating loins*"

Means (Instrument): The ablative expresses the means by which an action is accomplished:

    tectum <u>nullis vestibus</u>, "covered *by no clothing*"

Place Where: Often denoted by the preposition *in* along with the ablative; the preposition is commonly ommitted in poetry or poetic prose.

    templi <u>parietibus</u> tui notavi, "I noted *on the walls* of your temple"

Place From Which: The ablative denotes the place a noun has moved from usually with a preposition.

    gemmas <u>germine</u> exeuntes, "buds coming *from the sprout*"

Quality (description): Quality is regularly denoted by the ablative.

> *lumine est Venus paeto*, "Venus has a squinting eye"

Separation: Separation is expressed with or without a preposition especially with verbs and adjectives of deprivation, freedom, and want.

> *defectus pueroque feminaque*, "deprived *of boy and girl*"

Specification: The ablative of specification provides details with respect to which anything is or is done.

> *terribilem fuste*, "terrible *with a club*"

Time: Both time when and time within which are denoted by the ablative.

> *prima dat nocte*, "she gives *on the first night*"
>
> *nocte peregit una*, "she completed *in the course of one night*"

LOCATIVE

The locative case is used for the location of towns and small islands of first and second declension, *humus, domus, rus,* and sometimes countries and large islands as an alternative to ablative of place where.

> *cucumeresque humi fusos*, "cucumbers poured out *on the ground*"

Priapea

2. Uses of the Subjunctive

Independent Uses of the Subjunctive

Deliberative questions occur when the speaker wonders what he or she should do.

> *quid faciam?*: "What should I do?

Hortatory, Jussive, Prohibition Clauses:

Jussive and hortatory subjunctives "urges" some action in a more polite manner than an imperative. "Hortatory" applies to first person "let us…"); "jussive" applies to second and third person (may you…, let her…"); "prohibition" refers to the negative (don't…).

> *accedat*: "let him come!"
>
> *neque possis*: "may you not be able!"

The volitive subjunctive expresses a wish for the future:

> *periam*: "may I die!"

Dependent Uses of the Subjunctive

Tenses of the subjunctive in subordinate clauses follow the *sequence of tenses*: present or perfect subjunctive for primary sequence, imperfect or pluperfect for secondary sequence.

tense of main clause	same time or time after main verb	time before main verb
present or future tense	present subjunctive	perfect subjunctive
past tense	imperfect subjunctive	pluperfect subjunctive

Concessive clauses with *cum, quamvis* or *licet* take the subjunctive:

> *quamvis sim*: "although I am"
>
> *cum capiant*: "although they hold"
>
> *licet torqueas*: "although you twist your hair"

Conditions: The subjunctive is used in future less vivid and contrafactual conditions (see below)

Cum Causal Clauses: When *cum* introduces a causal clause, the subjunctive is used:

> *cum…luat*: "since you pay"

xxvi

Cum Circumstantial Clauses: When *cum* introduces a general circumstance rather than a specific time, the subjunctive is used

>*cum…ostendas*: "when you show"

Cum Temporal clauses referring to past actions in secondary sequence regularly take the subjunctive.

>*cum…pererrasset*: "when she had wandered"

Indirect commands are an example of a jussive noun clause used as the object of a verb. For more on jussive noun clauses, see below.

>*rogat temptes*: "she asks you to try"

Indirect questions are formed with the subjunctive following the sequence of tenses and introduced by an interrogative word.

>*dic mihi qua iter sit*: "tell me where your route is"

Noun Clauses clauses following certain verbs are introduced with our without *ut* or *ne* with the subjunctive, as in indirect commands:

>*quereris quod astem*: "why do you complain that I am standing"

Purpose Clauses explain the purpose behind the action of the main clause and is usually introduced by *ut* or *ne*.

>*tu quae averteris ne videas*: "you who look away in order not to see"

Relative Clauses of Characteristic: Relative clauses in the subjunctive suggest that that the clause does not simply state a fact but rather indicates another type of subjunctive clause such as purpose, result, cause, concession, etc. They are called relative clauses of characteristic for introducing a defining quality or characteristic.

>*tu quae averteris*: "you who are (the kind who) turn away"

Result clauses explain the outcome of the action in the main clause, often with an adverb in the main clause signalling the result clause. Result clauses are usually introduced by *ut* or *ut non*.

>*adeo plena ut putem*: "so full that I suppose"

3. Conditional sentences

Future more vivid conditions express a future *probability*. The protasis (the clause expressing the condition, i.e. the "if" clause) can be the future or future perfect, the apodosis (the clause expressing consequence, i.e. the "then" clause) is the future tense or some equivalent. In English this is expressed with the present tense in the protasis, future tense in the apodosis: "If she comes…then I will go."

> *si dederis, licebit*: "if you give, it will be permitted"

Future less vivid conditions express a future *possibility* and thus use the potential subjunctive in the apodosis and present or perfect subjunctive in the protasis; In English, "If it should…then it would…" or "If it were to…then it would."

> *si tractes, putes?*: "if you were to handle it, would you suppose?"

Contrafactual conditions indicate an untrue premise and conclusion and use the subjunctive mood: imperfect subjunctive for the present (i.e. "if he were now doing this, he would be doing badly"); pluperfect subjunctive for the past (i.e. "if he had done this, he would have done badly").

> *nisi placuisset, non habuisset*: "unless he had been pleasing, it would not have been necessary"

Mixed conditions are common, where a less vivid protasis is combined with an apodosis in the future indicative:

> *si telum desit, inermis ero*: "if the weapon were to be lacking, I will be unarmed"

C. Other terms used in the commentary

Anastrophe – the reversal of normal word order
> *mentulam ad* for *ad mentulam*

Hendiadys - ("one through two) the use of two nouns linked by a conjunction instead of a noun and adjective:
> *graculusve raptor*: "a jackdaw and plunderer" i.e. a plundering jackdaw

Litotes - (understatement) is the use of two negatives to produce a positive:
> *non nimium*: "not too much" i.e. a little

Other Terminology

Apocopation – when a word is formed by the removal of the end of a longer word

>*subripuere*: apoc. perf. (= *subripuerunt*)

Syncopation – the contraction of a word by omission of part of the middle

>*dicarunt*: syncopated perf. (= *dicaeverunt*)

Periphrastic: the use of a participle and a form of the verb esse to create a tense:

>*conspicuendus est Apollo*: (gerundive) "Apollo ought to be seen," lit. Apollo is one who ought to be seen

Priapea: Songs for a Phallic God

I   ELEGAIC COUPLETS

An address to the reader, this poem is a preamble to the whole collection.

Carminis incompti lusus lecture procaces,
    conveniens Latio pone supercilium.
non soror hoc habitat Phoebi, non Vesta sacello,
    nec quae de patrio vertice nata dea est,
sed ruber hortorum custos, membrosior aequo,   5
    qui tectum nullis vestibus inguen habet.

---

aequus, -a, -um: equal, usual
carmen, -inis *n*: song, verse
convenio (4): to be appropriate to
custos, -odis *m*: guard
dea, -ae *f*: goddess
habito (1): to inhabit, dwell live, stay
hortus, -i *m*: garden
incomptus, -a, -um: untidy, unpolished
inguen, -inis *n*: groin
Latium, -i: Latium, of Rome
lusus, -us *m*: jest
membrosus, -a, um: having a large member

nascor, nasci, natus sum: to be born
patrius, -a, -um: father's, paternal
pono (3): to lay aside
procax, -acis (*gen.*): impudent, undisciplined
ruber, -ra, -rum: red, ruddy
sacellum, -i *n*: shrine
soror, -is *f*: sister
supercilium, -i *n*: eyebrow, sternness
tego (3), **texi, tectus**: to cover
vertex, verticis *m*: crown of the head
Vesta, -ae *f*: Vesta, goddess of the hearth
vestis, -is *f*: clothing

lecture: fut. act. part. voc. of *lego* "you *about to read*"
conveniens: pres. part. neut. agreeing with *supercilium*, "appropriate to" + dat.
pone: imper., "lay aside!"
supercilium: raising the eyebrow showed disapproval, and thus can mean "sternness"
soror: the sister of Phoebus is the virgin goddess Diana
hoc ... sacello: abl. place where, "in this shrine"
de patrio vertice: Minerva was born parthenogenetically from the head of Jupiter
ruber custos: the "ruddy guard" is Priapus, who was painted red
aequo: abl. of comparison after *membrosior*, "larger-membered *than is usual*"
nullis vestibus: abl. of means, "covered *by no clothing*"

Priapea

aut igitur tunicam parti praetende tegendae,
aut quibus hanc oculis adspicis, ista lege.

---

aspicio (3): to look at, gaze on
oculus, -i *m*: an eye
pars, partis *f*: part

praetendo (3): to stretch out X (*acc.*) over Y (*dat.*)
tego (3): to cover
tunica, -ae *f*: undergarment, tunic

---

parti: dat. after *praetende* "stretch over *the part*"
tegendae: gerundive dat. agreeing with *parti*, "the part *that ought to be covered*"
quibus oculis: abl. of means "*by whichever eyes* you look"
hanc (sc. **partem**): "cover *this* part" i.e. his member
ista (sc. **carmina**): n. pl., "read *these* songs!"

II   HENDECASYLLABLE

Dedication to Priapus. This poem is another preamble to the whole collection, a dedication by the poet to Priapus.

Ludens haec ego teste te, Priape,
horto carmina digna, non libello,
scripsi non nimium laboriose.
nec Musas tamen, ut solent poetae,
ad non virgineum locum vocavi.   5
nam sensus mihi corque defuisset,
castas, Pierium chorum, sorores

---

carmen, -inis *n*: song, verse
castus, -a, -um: chaste
chorus, -i *m*: chorus
cor, -dis *n*: heart
desum, desse, defui: to be lacking, abandon (+ *dat.*)
dignus, -a –um: worthy of (+ *dat.*)
laboriose: laboriously
libellus, -i *m*: little book
locus, -i *m*: place
ludo (3): to play, mock, tease, trick

musa, -ae *f*: muse
Pierius, -a, -um: of Pieria, a region sacred to the Muses
poeta, -ae *m*: poet
scribo, -ere, scripsi: write
sensus, -us *m*: feeling, sense
soleo (2): to be accustomed
soror, -is *f*: sister
testis, -is *n*: witness
virgineus, -a, -um: pertaining to a virgin
voco (1): to call, invoke

---

teste te: abl. abs., "with you as witness"
horto ... libello: dat. after *digna*, "worthy *of a garden* ... not *a little book*"
non nimium: litotes, "not too much"
non virgineum: "not suitable for virgins"
defuisset: plupf. subj. in past contrafactual apodosis, "sense and heart *would have abandoned* me"
Pierium chorum: i.e. the Muses

auso ducere mentulam ad Priapi.
ergo quicquid id est, quod otiosus
templi parietibus tui notavi,
in partem accipias bonam, rogamus.

---

accipio (3): to accept
audeo (3), **ausi, ausus**: to dare (+ *inf.*)
bonus, -a, um: good
mentula, ae *f.*: penis (*obsc.*), "dick"
noto (1): to inscribe

otiosus, -a, -um: unoccupied, at leisure
paries, -tis *m*: wall
quisquid, quicquid: whatever
rogo (1): to ask
templum, -i *n*: temple

---

auso: perf. part. dat. of *audeo* agreeing with *mihi*, and representing a past contrafactual protasis, "*me having dared* to lead" i.e. if I had dared"
mentulam ad: anastrophe for "*ad mentulam*"
parietibus: abl. place, "on the walls"
accipias: pres. subj. in jussive noun clause after *rogamus*, "we ask *that you receive*"
in partem bonam: "in the good sense," i.e. favorably

III ELEGAIC COUPLETS

Priapus asks for favors in plain language

Obscure poteram tibi dicere: da mihi, quod tu
 des licet assidue, nil tamen inde perit.
da mihi, quod cupies frustra dare forsitan olim,
 cum tenet obsessas invida barba genas,
quodque Jovi dederat qui raptus ab alite sacra   5

---

ales, alitis *f.*: bird
assidue: continually
barba, -ae *f.*: beard
cupio (3): to desire
forsitan: perhaps
frustra: in vain
gena, -ae *f.*: cheeks
inde: therein

invidus, -a, -um: hostile, hated
licet: it is permitted, although (+ *subj.*)
obscure: secretly
obsideo (2) **obsedi, obsessus**: to beset, besiege
olim: hereafter
pereo (4), **perii, peritus**: to perish, diminish
rapio (3), **rapui, raptus**: to snatch, seize
sacer, sacra, -um: holy, sacred

---

quod... perit: rel. clause, "(that) *which diminishes* not at all"
des: pres. subj. concessive after *licet*, "although you give"
cupies: fut., "what *you will desire* (to give) in vain" + *inf.*, i.e. because no one will want it
invida barba: nom., the appearance of facial hair signaled the moment when a boy was no longer an appropriate object of desire
Jovi: dat. ind. obj., "he had given *to Jupiter*"
raptus: perf. part., "he who *having been snatched*" i.e. Ganymede
ab alite sacra: abl. of agent, "snatched *by the holy eagle*" i.e. of Jupiter

Priapea

    miscet amatori pocula grata suo,
quod virgo prima cupido dat nocte marito,
    dum timet alterius vulnus inepta loci.
simplicius multo est "da pedicare" Latine
    dicere. quid faciam? crassa Minerva mea est.   10

---

amator, -oris *m*: lover	**nox, noctis** *f*: night
crassus, -a, -um: crass, gross	**pedico** (1): to sodomize, "assfuck"
cupidus, -a, -um: desiring	**poculum, -i** *n*: cup
gratus, -a, -um: pleasing, welcome	**simplex, -icis** (*gen.*): simple, easy
ineptus, -a, -um: ignorant	**timeo** (2): to fear
maritus, -i *m*: husband	**virgo, -inis** *f*: virgin
misceo (2): to mix, stir up	**vulnus, -eris** *n*: wound

amatori ... suo: dat. of advantage, "who mixes *for his lover*" Ganymede became the wine server of Jupiter
prima ... nocte: abl. of time, "on the first night"
cupido marito: dat. ind. obj., "to her desiring husband"
alterius ... loci: gen. objective, "the wound *of the other place*" i.e. in the front
multo: abl. of degree of difference, "easier *by much*"
pedicare: inf. after *da*, "allow me *to penetrate from behind*"
dicere: epex. inf. after *simplicius*, "easier *to say*"
quid faciam?: pres. subj. in deliberative question, "What should I do?"
Minerva mea: "my craft" a metonymy, since Minerva is the goddess of craft, but ironic since Minerva was a virgin

An Invocation to Priapus. Marble bas-relief.
(National Archaeological Museum, Naples.)

Songs for a Phallic God

IV   HENDECASYLLABLE

An erotic picture book provides suggested positions

Obscenas rigido deo tabellas
ducens ex Elaphantidos libellis
dat donum Lalage rogatque, temptes,
si pictas opus edat ad figuras.

---

donum, **-i** *n*: gift
edo (3): to perform
Elephantis, -idos *f*: Elephantis
figura, -ae *f*: shape, form
Lalage, -es *f*: "Laughter," the name of a girl
libellus, -i *m*: little, small book
obscenus, -a, -um: obscene, lewd
opus, operis *n*: need, work
pictus, -a, -um: painted, colored
rigidus, -a, -um: stiff, hard
rogo (1): to ask
tabella, -ae *f*: document, letter
tempto (1): to try

---

rigido deo: dat. ind. obj., "gives *to the rigid god*" i.e. Priapus
Elaphantidos: a Roman poetess who produced a sex manual, referred to in Suetonius (Tibullus 43) and Martial (*Epigram.* 12, 43)
Lalage: for the Greek name cf. Horace, *Carm.* 1.22
temptes: pres. subj. in ind. com. after *rogat*, "asks you *to try*"
si edat: pres. subj. in indirect question after *temptes*, "test *whether she can perform*"
opus edat: the expression means to perform a sexual act or to publish a book.
pictas ... ad figuras: "according to the painted pictures"

V   ELEGAIC COUPLETS

Priapus makes a deal with a boy

Quam puero legem fertur dixisse Priapus,
    versibus his infra scripta duobus erit:
"quod meus hortus habet, sumas impune licebit,
    si dederis nobis, quod tuus hortus habet."

---

infra: below
inpune: without punishment
lex, legis *f*: law m
licet: it is permitted (+ *subj.*)
sumo (3): to take up obtain
versus, -us *m*: line, verse

---

puero: dat. of referenece, "the law *for the boy*"
dixisse: perf. inf. after *fertur*, "Priapus is reported *to have pronounced*"
scripta ... erit: future perf., "it will be written" i.e. the law
sumas: pres. subj. after *licebit*, "it will be permitted for you to take"
dederis: fut. perf. in future more vivid protasis, "if first *you will have given*"
tuus hortus: "your garden," i.e. your buttocks

Priapea

VI   HENDECASYLLABLE

Let the thief beware! One of a series of poems where Priapus threatens those who violate his garden.

> Quod sum ligneus, ut vides, Priapus
> et falx lignea ligneusque penis,
> prendam te tamen et tenebo prensum
> totamque hanc sine fraude, quantacunque est,
> tormento citharaque tensiorem   5
> ad costam tibi septimam recondam.

---

cithara, -ae *f*: cithara, a stringed instrument
costa, -ae *f*: side, rib
falx, falcis *f*: a sickle
fraus, -dis *f*: deceit
ligneus, -a, -um: wooden

prendo (3), **prendi, prensus**: to take, grasp
quantacunque: however great
recondo (3): to bury (by inserting)
tensus, -a, -um: tight, stiff
tormentum, -i *n*: a catapult

Quod sum: concessive, "although I am"
prensum: perf. part. agreeing with *te*, "hold you *having been taken*"
totamque hanc (sc. **mentulam**): "*this whole* (*mentulam*) I will bury"
tormento citharaque: abl. of comp. after *tensiorem*, "tighter than *a catapult and a cithara*"
ad costam septimam: "all the way up to your seventh rib"

VII   ELEGAIC COUPLET

A word play on "pedico"

> Cum loquor, una mihi peccatur littera: nam "Te
> Pe dico" semper blaesaque lingua mihi est.

---

blaesus, -a, -um: mispronouncing
lingua, -ae *f*: tongue
littera, -ae *f*: letter (of the alphabet)

loquor, loqui, locutus sum: to speak
pecco (1): to be wrong, mispronounce

This couplet is a letter game. Priapus mistakenly inserts "pe" where he meant to say "te," producing the word *pedico* instead of *te dico*.
blaesaque: nom. pred., "and my tongue is *mispronouncing*"

VIII   HENDECASYLLABLE

Married woman like to read these poems too

> Matronae procul hinc abite castae,
> turpe est vos legere impudica verba.
> non assis faciunt euntque recta:
> nimirum sapiunt videntque magnam
> matronae quoque mentulam libenter.   5

abeo, abire: to depart, go away	**matrona, -ae** *f*: wife matron
as, assis *m*: copper coin	**mentula, -ae** *f*: penis (*obsc.*), "dick"
castus, -a, -um: chaste	**procul**: away
hinc: hence	**nimirum**: no wonder
impudicus, -a, -um: unchaste	**recta** (*adv.*): directly
lego (2): to read	**sapio** (3): to be wise, understand
libenter: willingly	**turpis, -e**: disgraceful indecent

abite: imper., "you go away!"
legere: pres. inf. epexegetic after *turpe*, "indecent for you *to read*"
assis: gen. of price "for even an *as*" (a very small sum)
faciunt euntque (sc. **matronae**) **recta**: "*they don't do* (as I say) *and go directly* (to the *impudica verba*)"
sapiunt: "they are knowledgeable"

IX   ELEGAIC COUPLETS

Priapus is as proud of his member as the other gods are of their special characteristics

> Cur obscena mihi pars sit sine veste, requiris?
>   quaere, tegat nullus cur sua tela deus.
> fulmen habens mundi dominus tenet illud aperte,
>   nec datur aequoreo fuscina tecta deo.

aequoreus, -a, -um: connected with the sea	**pars, -tis** *f*: part
aperte: openly, publicly	**quaero** (3): to ask
cur: why?	**requiro** (3): to seek, ask
dominus, -i *m*: owner, lord, master	**tectus, -a, -um**: hidden, secret
fulmen, -inis *n*: lightning	**tego** (3): to cover
fuscina, -ae *f*: trident	**telum, -i** *n*: weapon
mundus, -i *m*: world	**vestis, -is** *f*: clothing
obscenus, -a, -um: indecent, obscene	

cur ... sit: pres. subj. in ind. question after *requiris*, "you ask *why it is*"
tegat: pres. subj. in ind. question after *quaere*, "ask why no god *covers*"
dominus: i.e. Jupiter
aequoreo deo: i.e. Neptune

Priapea

nec Mavors illum, per quem valet, occulit ensem,   5
   nec latet intrepidae Palladis hasta sinu.
num pudet auratas Phoebum portare sagittas?
   clamne solet pharetram ferre Diana suam?
num tegit Alcides nodosae robora clavae?
   sub tunica virgam num deus ales habet?   10
quis Bacchum gracili vestem praetendere thyrso,
   quis te celata cum face vidit, Amor?
nec mihi sit crimen, quod mentula semper aperta est:
   hoc mihi si telum desit, inermis ero.

---

ales, alitis (*gen.*): winged
apertus, -a, -um: uncovered
auratus, -a, -um: golden
Bacchus, -i *m*: Bacchus, god of wine
celo (1): to conceal
clam: secretly
clava, -ae *f*: club
crimen, -inis *n*: crime
desum, deesse: to be wanting, lacking
Diana, -ae *f*: Diana, goddess of the hunt
ensis, ensis *m*: sword
fax, facis *f*: torch
fero, ferre: to carry
gracilis, -e: slender
hasta, -ae *f*: spear
inermis, -e: unarmed
intrepidus, -a, -um: fearless
lateo (2): to lie hidden

Mavors, Mavortis *m*: Mars, god of war
nodosus, -a, -um: knotty
occulo (3): to hide, conceal
Pallas, -adis *f*: Pallas Athena, Minerva
pharetra, -ae *f*: quiver
porto (1): to carry
praetendo (3): to stretch X (*acc.*) over Y (*dat.*)
pudeo (2): to be ashamed
robus, roboris *n*: oak
sagitta, -ae *f*: arrow
sinus, -us *m*: fold (of cloth)
telum, -i *n*: weapon
thyrsus, -i *m*: Bacchic wand tipped with a fir-cone
tunica, -ae *f*: tunic
valeo (2): to be powerful
vestis, -is *f*: clothing
virga, -ae *f*: staff

Palladis: i.e. of Minerva
sinu: abl. place, "*in the cloak* of Pallas"
pudet: impersonal, "it is not a shame, is it?" + *acc.* + *inf.*
Alcides: nom., "descendant of Alceus" i.e. Hercules
nodosae … clavae: gen. of description, "of his knotty club"
deus ales: "the winged god" i.e. Mercury
virgam: Mercury carries the *caduceus*, with which he closes the eyes of the dead
gracili … thyrso: dat. after *praetendere*, "stretch clothing over *the slender thyrsus*"
praetendere: pres. inf. after *vidit*, who sees Bacchus *to stretch*"
celata cum face: abl. of circumstance, "with a hidden torch" a common attribute of Amor
nec sit: jussive subj., "nor let it be"
si desit: pres. subj. in future less vivid protasis, "if it were to be lacking"

Songs for a Phallic God

X

HENDECASYLLABLES

A rustic admires Priapus

Insulsissima quid puella rides?
non me Praxiteles Scopasve fecit,
non sum Phidiaca manu politus,
sed lignum rude vilicus dolavit
et dixit mihi: "tu Priapus esto." 5
spectas me tamen et subinde rides?
nimirum tibi salsa res videtur
adstans inguinibus columna nostris.

---

adsto (1): to stand erect
columna, -ae *f.*: a column (= *mentula*)
dolo (1): to chip with an ax, hew
inguen, -inis *n*: the loins
insulsus, -a, -un: tasteless, awkward
lignum, -i *n*: piece of wood
manus, -us *f.*: a hand
nimirum (*adv.*): no wonder

polio (4): to polish
rideo (2): to smile at
rudis, -e: rough, rude
salsus, -a, -um: salty, witty
specto (1): to look at
subinde: repeatedly
vilicus, -i *m*: a rustic person

Praxiteles, Scopas, Phidias: famous sculptors
Phidiacia manu: abl. of means, "with the hand of Phidias"
dolavit: literally, "hewed me," with an obscene connotation
esto: 3 s. imper., "*may it be* Priapus!" he (the sculptor) said
salsa res: predicate with *videtur*, "seems to be *a witty thing*"
inguinibus nostris: abl. of place from which, "from our loins"

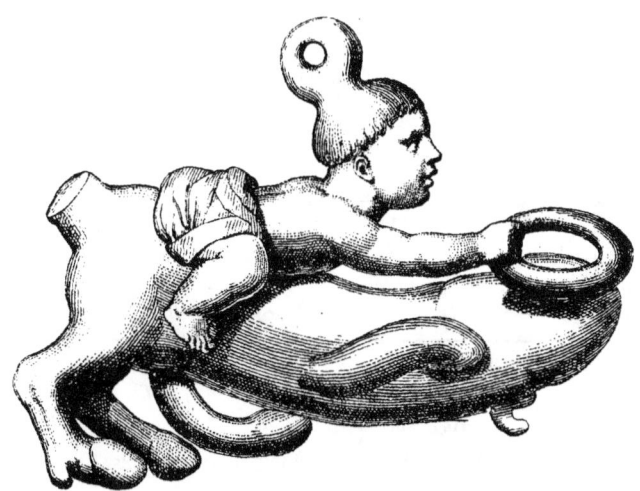

Jockey riding and crowning a winged phallus. Bronze *tintinnabulum* (wind chime), c. 1st century CE. From Pompeii. (National Archaeological Museum, Naples.)

Priapea

XI ELEGIAC COUPLETS

Let the thief beware!

> Ne prendare cave. prenso nec fuste nocebo,
> saeva nec incurva vulnera falce dabo:
> trajectus conto sic extendere pedali,
> ut culum rugam non habuisse putes.

caveo (2): to beware	**prendo** (3), **prendi, prensus**: to catch
contus, -i *m*: a pole (=*mentula*)	**puto** (1): to suppose
culus, -i *m*: anus, "ass(hole)"	**saevus, -a, -um**: savage
falx, falcis *f*: a sickle	**trajicio** (3) **-jeci, -jectus**: to pass through, penetrate
fustis, -is *m*: a club	**ruga, -ae** *f*: wrinkle
incurvus, -a, -um: curved	**vulnus, -eris** *n*: wound
noceo (2): to harm	
pedalis, -e: foot-long	

ne prendare: pres. subj. 2nd s. pass. in noun clause after *cave*, "take care *lest you be caught*"
prenso: perf. part. dat. after *nocebo*, "harm you *having been caught*"
fuste: abl. means, "harm *with my club*"
incurva falce: abl. of means, "wound *with my curved sickle*"
trajectus: "you *having been penetrated*"
extendere: fut. 2 s. pass., "you will be stretched"
ut non putes: pres. subj. in result clause, "so that you will not suppose"
habuisse: perf. inf. after *putes*, "that your ass *had*" i.e. because it will be so stretched

XII HENDECASYLLABLE

A diatribe against an old woman

> Quaedam serior Hectoris parente,
> Cumaeae soror, ut puto, Sibyllae,
> aequalis tibi, quam domum revertens

aequalis, -e: equal, similar to (+ *dat*.)	**revertor** (3): to return
domus, -i *f*: house, building	**serior, -ius**: older
Hector, -oris *m*: Hector, the Trojan hero	**Sibylla, -ae** *f*: prophetess, sibyl
parens, -entis *f*: parent	**soror, -is** *f*: sister

quaedam: nom., "a certain woman"
parente: abl. of comparison after *serior*, "older *than the mother of Hector*" i.e. Hecuba, who is often cited as a typical old woman
Cumaeae Sibyllae: the Sybil of Cumae was a legendary old hag
ut puto: parenthetical, "so I believe"
quam: antecedent is *tibi*, "same age as you *whom*" addressing Hecale, another legendary old woman. She helped Theseus, but was found dead by him upon his return.

Songs for a Phallic God

Theseus repperit in rogo jacentem,
infirmo solet huc gradu venire   5
rugosasque manus ad astra tollens,
ne desit sibi mentula, rogare.
hesterna quoque luce dum precatur,
dentem de tribus excreavit unum.
"tolle" inquam "procul et jube latere   10
scissa sub tunica stolaque russa,
ut semper solet, et timere lucem,
qui tanto patet indecens hiatu,

---

astrum, -i *n*: star	**lux, lucis** *f*: light
dens, dentis *m*: tooth	**pateo** (2): to stand open, be open
desum, desse: to be absent	**precor** (1): to pray, supplicate, beseech
excreo (1): to cough up	**procul** (*adv.*): at distance, far off
gradus, -us *m*: position	**reperio** (4), **repperi, repertus**: to discover
hesternus, -a, -um: of yesterday	**rogo** (1): to ask
hiatus, -us *m*: opening, fissure	**rogus, -i** *m*: funeral pyre
huc: hither	**rugosus, -a, -um**: full of wrinkles
indecens, -entis (*gen.*): indecent	**russus, -a, -um**: red
infirmus, -a, -um: fragile, frail, feeble	**scindo** (3), **scidi, scissus**: to tear, split, divide
inquam: to say	**stola, -ae** *f*: stola
jaceo (2): to lie prostrate	**timeo** (2): to fear
jubeo (2): to order, tell, command, direct	**tollo** (3): to lift, raise, take
lateo (2): to lie hidden, lurk	**tunica, -ae** *f*: tunic, undergarment

solet: the subject is *quaedam* from the first verse, "she *is accustomed* to come"
infirmo … gradu: abl. of manner, "with a weak gait"
rogare: inf. also complementing *solet*, "is accustomed *to ask*"
ne desit: ind. command after *rogare*, "ask that my mentula *not be absent*" + dat.
hesterna luce: abl. of time, "yesterday"
de tribus: "one tooth *from the three*"
tolle procul: "take far away"
latere: inf. after *jube*, "order it *to hide*" the object of both verbs is the antecedent of *qui* below, referring to the old woman's genitals
stola: this is the outer garment of a dignified woman
ut semper solet: parenthetical, "as is its usual custom"
timere: pres. inf. after *jube*, "order it to *fear* the light"
qui patet: the antecedent is the object of *jube* and subject of *latere* and *timere*, "that which lies open"
hiatu: abl. of specification, indecent *in gap*"

> barbato macer eminente naso,
> ut credas Epicuron oscitari." 15

barbatus, -a, -um: bearded	**nasus, -i** *m*: nose
emineo (2): to stand out be prominent	**Epicurus, -i** *m*: Epicurus, the philosopher
macer, macra, -um,: scraggy	**oscito** (1): to gape, yawn

macer: in apposition to *qui*, "all scraggy"
eminente naso: abl. of circumstance, "with a prominent nose" an obscene term for a penis or, as here, for a clitoris
ut credas: pres. subj. in result clause, "so that you would believe"
Epicuron oscitari: ind. st. after *credas*, "that Epicurus is yawning" It is not clear why the old woman's genitals resemble Epicurus' yawning mouth, but there are other references to the "yawn" of Epicurus

XIII ELEGAIC COUPLETS

Let the thief beware!

> Percidere, puer, moneo: futuere, puella:
> barbatum furem tertia poena manet.

barbatus, -a, -um: bearded	**maneo** (2): to await
fur, furis *m*: thief	**moneo** (3): to remind, advise, warn
futuo (3): to screw, fuck	**percido** (3): to assault, to sodomize

percidere: syncopated 2 s. fut. pass. (=*percideris*) "you will be sodomized"
moneo: parenthetical, "I warn you"
futuere: syncopated 2 s. fut. pass (=*futueris*), "you will be screwed"
tertia poena: i.e. the third punishment is *irrumatio*
barbatum furem: "a bearded thief" having a beard indicates manhood, hence the use of another orifice for punishment from the boy or girl

XIV HENDECASYLLABLE

All are welcome in the garden of Priapus, even if tainted by sin

> Huc huc, quisquis es, in dei salacis
> deverti grave ne puta sacellum.

deverto (3): to turn away	**sacellum, -i** *n*: a little shrine
gravis, -e: serious	**salax, salacis** (*gen.*): lecherous

deverti: pres. pass. inf. after *puta*, "don't suppose *that you are turned away*"
in...sacellum: acc. showing motion towards, "hither *into the shrine*"

et si nocte fuit puella tecum,
hac re quod metuas adire, non est.
istud caelitibus datur severis: 5
nos vappae sumus et pusilla culti
ruris numina, nos pudore pulso
stamus sub Jove coleis apertis.
ergo quilibet huc licebit intret
nigri fornicis oblitus favilla. 10

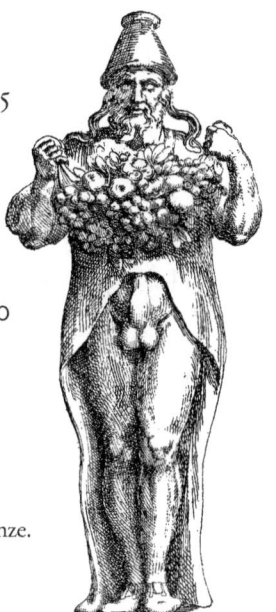

Priapus bearing fruit. Engraving after Roman bronze. Pietro Santi Bartoli (*Museum Odescalchum, sive, Thesaurus antiquarum gemmarum*, 1751.)

adeo (4): to approach
apertus, -a, -um: open
caeles, caelitis *m*: a heaven-dweller, god
coleus, -i *m*: sack; (*pl.*) testicles, "balls"
cultor (1): to worship
favilla, -ae *f*: glowing ashes, embers spark
fornix, -icis *m*: brothel
intro (1): to enter
licet: it is permitted (+ *subj.*)
metuo (3): to fear

niger, nigra, -um: black, dark unlucky
numen, -inis *n*: divine power
oblino (3), **oblitum**: to stain
pello (3), **pepuli, pulsus**: to drive
pudor, -oris *m*: shame
pusillus, -a, -um: insignificant
quilibet, quaelibet, quodlibet: anyone
rus, ruris *n*: the country, farm
severus, -a, -um: severe
vappa, -ae *m*: a worthless person

nocte: abl. of time, "at night"
hac re: abl. of cause, "for this reason" i.e. because you were with a girl last night
non est: "it is not the case"
quod ... metuas: pres. subj. in noun clause subject of *non est*, "it is not the case *that you should fear*" + inf.
istud: nom. subject, "*that kind* (of reverence)"
caelitibus severis: dat. ind. obj., "given to the severe gods"
culti (sc. **sumus**): "and we have worshiped"
pudore pulso: abl. abs., "shame having been driven away"
sub Jove: metonymy, "under the sky"
coleis apertis: abl. of circumstance, "with bare balls"; note the resemblance to the common phrase *coelis apertis*, "open skies"
intret: pres. subj. after *licebit*, "he will be permitted *to enter*"
oblitus: perf. part. concessive, "although stained"
favilla: abl. of means, "stained *by the ash*"
nigri fornicis: gen. after *favilla*, "ash *of a black whorehouse*"

Priapea

XV

HENDECASYLLABLE

Let the thief beware

Commisso mihi non satis modestas
quicunque attulerit manus agello,
is me sentiet esse non spadonem.
dicat forsitan haec sibi ipse: "nemo
hic inter frutices loco remoto   5
percisum sciet esse me", sed errat:
magnis testibus ista res agetur.

---

affero (3): to lay X (*acc.*) upon Y (*dat.*)
agellus, -i *m*: a little field
committo (3), **-misi, -missus**: to entrust
erro (1): to make a mistake, err
forsitan: perhaps
frutex, fruticis *m*: shrub, bush
modestus, -a, -um: modest
percido (3), **percidi, percisus**: to assault, sodomize

quicunque, quaecunque, quodcunque: whoever
remotus, -a, -um: remote
satis: enough
scio (4): to know, understand
sentio (3): to perceive, feel, sense
spado, -nis *m*: eunuch
testis, -is m (1): witness
testis, -is m (2): testicle

---

commisso: perf. part. dat. modifying *agello*, "the garden *having been charged* to me"
non satis modestas: litotes, "*immodest* hands"
attulerit: fut. perf. in relative conditional clause, "whoever (if anyone) touches"
me esse: ind. st. after *sentiet*, "he will sense *that I am*"
spadonem: acc. pred., "that I am not a *eunuch*"
dicat: pres. subj. potential, "he might say"
loco remoto: abl. place where, "in this remote place" i.e., *agello*
percisum esse: perf. pass. inf. in ind. st. after *sciet*, "know *that I have been assaulted*"
magnis testibus: abl. of circumstance or means, "done *with great witnesses* or done *with great testicles*"
agetur: fut., "this *will be done*" or "this case will be tried"

Bacchanalia scene. White marble sarcophagus, 140-160 CE.
(National Archaeological Museum, Naples.)

XVI — ELEGAIC COUPLETS

Apples offered to Priapus

Qualibus Hippomenes rapuit Schoeneida pomis,
    qualibus Hesperidum nobilis hortus erat,
qualia credibile est spatiantem rure paterno
    Nausicaam pleno saepe tulisse sinu,
quale fuit malum, quod littera pinxit Aconti,   5
    qua lecta est cupido pacta puella viro:
taliacunque pius dominus florentis agelli
    imposuit mensae, nude Priape, tuae.

Acontius, -i *m*: Acontius
agellus, -i *m*: little field
credibilis, -e: credible
cupidus, -a, -um: eager, passionate
floreo (2): to flourish
hortus, i *f*: a garden
impono (3), **imposui, impositus**: to impose, put upon
littera, -ae *f*: letter
malum, -i *n*: fruit
mensa, -ae *f*: table course
nobilis, -e: noble
nudus, -a, -um: nude bare, stripped

paternus, -a, -um: paternal ancestral
pingo (3), **pinxi, pictus**: to paint
plenus, -a, -um: full
pacisco (3), **pactus sum**: to make an agreement, enter into a marriage contract with (+ *dat*.)
pius, -a, -um: upright, faithful
pomum, -i *n*: fruit
rapio (3), **rapui, raptus**: to snatch
rus, ruris *n*: country, farm
sinus, -us *m*: fold (of cloth), lap
spatior (1): to walk

Qualibus ... pomis: abl. of means, "with this sort of apples"
Hippomenes: nom. s., Hippomenes successfully wooed Atalanta with golden apples
Schoeneida: acc. s., "daughter of Schoeneus" i.e Atalanta
qualibus (sc. **pomis**): abl. of descr. after *nobilis*, "nobile *with such apples*"
Hesperidum: gen. pl., the Hesperides tended a fabulous garden with golden fruit
qualia (sc. **poma**): acc. obj. of *tulisse*, "to have carried *such fruits*"
rure paterno: abl. of place where, "walking *on her ancestral farm*"
tulisse: perf. inf. epexegetic after *credibile*, "it is credible for Nausicaa *to have carried*", Nausicaa helps Odysseus in *Odyssey 6*.
Aconti: the "letter" of Acontius was painted on a quince and read by his beloved, Cydippe, see Ovid, *Heroides 20-21*
qua: abl. of means, "the letter *by which*"
lecta: perf. part. also abl., "by which *having been read*"
est...pacta: perf. dep., "the girl *entered into a marriage with*" + dat.
taliacunque: acc. neut. pl. correlative with the various forms of *qualis* above, "such things"
mensae tuae: dat. after *imposuit*, "has placed on *your table*"

Priapea

XVII   HENDECASYLLABLE

Allow the thief to come!

> Quid mecum tibi, circitor moleste?
> ad me quid prohibes venire furem?
> accedat, sine: laxior redibit.

accedo (3): to come near, approach	**prohibeo** (2): to hinder, restrain forbid, prevent
circitor, -oris *m*: overseer	**redeo** (4): to return, go back, give back
laxus, -a, -um: breached, wide open	**sino** (3): to allow, permit
molestus, -a, -um: nasty, annoying	

tibi: dat. of interest, "what (concern is there) to you?"
venire: inf. in noun clause after *prohibes*, "prevent the thief *from coming*"
accedat: jussive subj., "let him come"
laxior: "more opened" i.e. from being penetrated

Figurine pitcher in the form of a Priapic dwarf.
Terra cotta, 1st century CE. From Herculaneum.
(National Archaeological Museum, Naples.)

XVIII   ELEGAIC COUPLETS

Size matters

> Commoditas haec est in nostro maxima pene,
> laxa quod esse mihi femina nulla potest.

commoditas, -atis *f*: timeliness fitness, aptness	**laxus, -a, -um**: loose
femina, -ae *f*: woman female	**maximus, -a, -um**: greatest
	penis, penis *m*: a penis

laxa: nom. pred., "no woman can be *loose* for me"
quod potest: noun clause in apposition to *commoditas*, "this advantage, *namely that* no woman *can*"

18

XIX   HENDECASYLLABLE

Telethusa's dancing is a turn-on

Hic quando Telethusa circulatrix,
quae clunem tunica tegente nulla
excitatius altiusque motat,
crisabit tibi fluctuante lumbo.
haec sic non modo te, Priape, possit,   5
privignum quoque sed movere Phaedrae.

---

altus, -a, -um: high deep
circulatrix, -atricis *f*: female itinerant performer
clunis, clunis *f*: buttock
criso (1): to move the haunches as in copulation
excitatus, -a, -um: excited
exsero (3), **exserui, exsertus**: to thrust out
fluctuo (1): to rise in waves, undulate
lumbus, -i *m*: loins
moto (1): to shake, stir
privignus, -i *m*: stepson
quando: when
tego (2): to cover, protect
tunica, -ae *f*: undergarment

Telethusa: a wanton dancer with the same name is mentioned in Martial 6.71.
tunica tegente: abl. abs., "with no tunic covering"
excitatius altiusque: acc. adverbial, "more excitedly and higher"
fluctuante lumbo: abl. of manner, "with undulating loins"
haec: i.e. Telethusa
possit: pres. subj. pot., "this girl *could*" + inf.
non modo ... quoque sed: "not only ... but even"
privignum ... Phaedra: "the stepson of Phaedra" i.e. Hippolytus, famously despising love.

XX   ELEGAIC COUPLETS

Like the other gods, Priapus has his weapon

Fulmina sub Jove sunt, Neptuni fuscina telum,
    ense potens Mars est, hasta, Minerva, tua est,

---

ense, ensis *m*: sword
fulmen, fulminis *n*: lightning
fuscina, -ae *f*: trident
hasta, -ae *f*: spear, lance, javelin
potens: powerful, strong
telum, -i *n*: dart, weapon

---

sub Jove: "under the command of Jupiter"
telum: nom. pred., "the trident *is the weapon* of Neptune"
Mars ... Minerva: vocatives, "is yours, *Mars ... Minerva*

Priapea

sutilibus Liber committit proelia thyrsis,
 fertur Apollinea missa sagitta manu,
Herculis armata est invicti dextera clava: 5
 at me terribilem mentula tenta facit.

armo, (1): to equip	**proelium**, **-i** *n*: battle
clava, **-ae** *f*: club	**sagitta**, **-ae** *f*: arrow
committo (3): to engage (in battle)	**sutilis**, **-e**: consisting of things stitched together
dextera, **-ae** *f*: right hand	
invictus, **-a**, **-um**: invincible	**tendo** (3), **tetendi**, **tentus**: to stretch
Liber, **Libri** *m*: Bacchus	**terribilis**, **-e**: frightful, terrible
mitto (3), **misi**, **missus**: to throw, hurl	**thyrsus**, **-i** *m*: Bacchic wand

sutilibus thyrsis: abl. of circumstance, "with stitched together wands"
fertur: "the arrow *is said*"
missa (sc. **esse**): impers. ind. st. after *fertur*, "the arrow is said *to be sent*"
Apollinea manu: abl. of means, "by Apollo's hand"
Herculis: gen., "the right hand *of Hercules*"
clava: abl. of means, "armed *with the club*"
terribilem: acc. pred., "makes me *terrible*"

Phallus in the form of a winged lion.
Bronze *tintinnabulum* (wind chime), c. 1st century CE.
From Pompeii. (National Archaeological Museum, Naples.)

XXI — ELEGIAC COUPLETS

Don't betray me, Priapus!

> Copia me perdit: tu suffragare rogatus,
>   indicio nec nos prode, Priape, tuo,
> quaeque tibi posui tamquam vernacula poma,
>   de Sacra nulli dixeris esse via.

---

copia, -ae *f*: plenty, abundance	**prodo, prodere**: bring forth, publish, reveal, betray
indicium, -i *n*: evidence (before a court) information, proof indication	**rogo** (1): to ask
perdo (3): to ruin, destroy lose waste	**suffrago** (1): to express support
pono (3), **posui**: to put, place	**vernaculus**, -a, -um: domestic, homegrown

---

Copia me perdit: "plenty has destroyed me" if the speaker is a prostitute, this suggest that her success is becoming a problem. Other commentators suggest that the speaker is the landowner, a thief, or a priest.

rogatus: perf. part. with conditional force, "*if you should be asked* to lend support"

indicio tuo: abl. of means, "with your evidence"

nec prode: imper. in prohibition, "*don't betray us*"

quaeque … poma: acc. obj. of *posui*, "*whatever apples* I have placed"

tamquam vernacula: "as if from my farm"

nulli: dat. ind. obj., "say *to no one*"

dixeris: perf. subj. in apodosis of a future less vivid condition, "you should say"

esse: pres. inf. in ind. st. after *dixeris*, "say them *to be*"

de Sacra via: i.e. that s/he bought them from the Sacra via rather than brought them from his farm, perhaps because this street was a red-light district

XXII — ELEGIAC COUPLET

Everyone has something for Priapus

> Femina si furtum faciet mihi virve puerve,
>   haec cunnum, caput hic praebeat, ille nates.

---

caput, -itis *n*: head i.e. the mouth	**furtum**, -i *n*: theft
cunnus, -i *m*: female genitalia (*obsc.*), "cunt"	**natis**, natis *f*: buttocks (*pl.*), rump
femina, -ae *f*: woman female	**praebeo** (2): to present, expose

---

si faciet: fut. in future more vivid protasis, "if a woman does"

mihi: dat. of advantage, "do a theft *to me*" i.e. steal "from me"

virve puerve: "or if man or boy"

praebeat: jussive subj. taking the place of fut. more vivid apodosis, "let this one expose"

Priapea

XXIII
HENDECASYLLABLE

A curse on thieves

> Quicunque hic violam rosamve carpet
> furtivumve holus aut inempta poma,
> defectus pueroque feminaque
> hac tentigine, quam videtis in me,
> rumpatur, precor, usque mentulaque 5
> nequiquam sibi pulset umbilicum.

---

carpo (3): to pluck	**precor** (3): to beg, pray
deficio (3), **defeci**, **defectus**: to deprive, be lacking (+ *abl*.)	**pulso** (1): to beat, pulsate
	rosa, -ae *f*: a rose
furtivus, -a, -um: furtive, secret	**rumpo**, (3), **rupi**, **ruptus**: to break burst
holus, holeris *n*: vegetables	**tentigo, tentiginis** *f*: tension, lust
inemptus, -a, -um: not bought, stolen	**umbilicus, -i** *m*: navel
nequiquam: in vain	**viola, -ae** *f*: a violet
pomum, -i *n*: a fruit	

---

carpet: pres. subj. in future less vivid protasis, "whoever (i.e. if someone) *were to pluck*"
pueroque feminaque: abl. of sep. after *defectus*, "deprived *of boy and girl*"
defectus: perf. part. agreeing with subject of *rumpatur*, "having been deprived"
hac tentigine: abl. of means, "burst *by this lust*"
rumpatur: pres. subj. jussive, "let him be burst"
precor: parenthetical, "I pray"
pulset: pres. subj. jussive, "let his *mentula* pulsate"

XXIV
ELEGAIC COUPLETS

Let the thief beware

> Hic me custodem fecundi vilicus horti
>   mandati curam jussit habere loci.

---

cura, -ae *f*: concern, worry	**jubeo**, (3), **jussi**, **jussus**: to order
custos, custodis *m*: guard	**locus, -i** *m*: position, place
fecundus, -a, -um: fertile	**mando** (1): to command, assign
hortus, -i *m*: garden	**vilicus, -i** *m*: farm overseer

---

custodem: acc. pred., "me to be *a guard*"
me habere: ind. st. after *jussit*, "ordered *me to have* a care"
mandati: perf. part. gen. agreeing with *loci*, "of this place *having been assigned* to me"

fur habeas poenam, licet indignere "feram"que
"propter holus" dicas "hoc ego?" propter holus.

---

holus, holeris *n*: vegetables
indignor (1): to deem unworthy

poena, -ae *f*: punishment
propter: because of, on account of (+ *acc.*)

habeas: pres. subj. jussive, "*may you have* this punishment"
indignere: pres. subj. 2 s. after *licet*, "although *you deem it unworthy*"
feram: fut., "*will I endure* this (punishment)?
propter holus: i.e. will I endure this *just for stealing vegetables*?
dicas: pres. subj. also after *licet*, "and although you say"

XXV   HENDECASYLLABLE

Priapus' "scepter" is also an instrument of punishment

Hoc sceptrum, quod ab arbore est recisum
nulla jam poterit virere fronde,
sceptrum, quod pathicae petunt puellae,
quod quidam cupiunt tenere reges,
cui dant oscula nobiles cinaedi,   5
intra viscera furis ibit usque
ad pubem capulumque coleorum.

---

arbor, -ris *f*: tree
capulus, -i *m*: sword-hilt, handle
cinaedus, -i *m*: catamite, pervert
coleus, -i *m*: sack; (*pl.*) testicles, "balls"
cupio (3): to desire (+ *inf.*)
frons, frondis *f*: foliage
fur, furis *m*: a theif
nobilis, -e: noble, well born
osculum, -i *n*: a kiss

pathicus, -a, -um: perverse
peto (3): to seek for
pubes, pubis *f*: pubic hair
recido, (3), recidi, recisus: to cut back
rex, regis *m*: king
sceptrum, -i *n*: scepter (= *mentula*)
teneo (2): to hold
vireo (3): to be green or lively
viscer, visceris *n*: entrails

nulla fronde: abl. of circumstance, "be green *with no leaves*" i.e. will never sprout again, parodying an epic phrase (e.g. *Aen.* 12.206, *Iliad* 1.234-6)
reges: punning on the literal meaning of *sceptrum*, a royal scepter
capulum coleorum: "up to *the handle of my testicles*," i.e. to his mentula

Priapea

XXVI

HENDECASYLLABLE

Priapus pleads with Romans not to wear him out with sex

> Porro - nam quis erit modus? - Quirites,
> aut praecidite seminale membrum,
> quod totis mihi noctibus fatigant
> vicinae sine fine prurientes
> vernis passeribus salaciores, 5
> aut rumpar, nec habebitis Priapum.
> ipsi cernitis, effututus ut sim
> confectusque macerque pallidusque,
> qui quondam ruber et valens solebam
> fures caedere quamlibet valentes. 10
> defecit latus et periculosam
> cum tussi miser exspuo salivam.

---

caedo (3): to cut down, sodomize
cerno (3):, to discern, see
conficio (3), **confeci, confectus**: to make, do thoroughly
deficio (3), **defeci, defectus**: to fail
effutuo (3), **effutui, effututus**: to wear out with sexual intercourse
expuo (3): to spit out
fatigo (1): to importune, wear out
finis, finis *m*: end, limit
latus, lateris *n*: flank, member (= *mentula*)
macer, -ra, -rum: thin, scraggy
membrum, -i *n*: member, organ
modus, -i *m*: bound, limit
pallidus, -a, -um: pale, yellow-green
passer, passeris *m*: sparrow

periculosus, -a, -um: dangerous
porro: furthermore
praecido (3): to cut short, limit
prurio (4): to have sexual craving
quamlibet: however much, any
Quiris, Quiritis *m*: citizens (*pl.*) of Rome
quondam: formerly, once
ruber, -ra, -rum: red
rumpo (3): to break destroy
salax, salacis (*gen.*): lecherous, lustful
saliva, -ae *f*: spittle
seminalis, -e: seed-bearing
tussis, tussis *n*: cough
valens -entis (**gen**): healthy
vernus, -a, -um: of spring, vernal
vicina, -ae *f*: a neighbor woman

---

totis noctibus: abl. of time, "importune me *so many nights*"
passeribus: abl. of comparison, "more lustful *than sparrows*"
rumpar: fut. pass., "I will be burst"
effututus ut sim confectusque: perf. subj. in noun clause following *cernitis*, "you perceive *that I am worn out and made* thin and pale"
qui (sc. **esse**) **solebam**: rel. clause, "I *who was accustomed (to be)* red and healthy"
caedere: pres. inf. complementing *solebam*, "who was accustomed *to cut down* thieves"
periculosam: "*dangerous* saliva" because a sign of illness
cum tussi: abl. of circumstance, "I spit *with a cough*"

Songs for a Phallic God

XXVII ELEGAIC COUPLETS

A dedication from Quintia

> Deliciae populi, magno notissima circo
>   Quintia, vibratas docta movere nates,
> cymbala cum crotalis, pruriginis arma, Priapo
>   ponit et adducta tympana pulsa manu:
> pro quibus, ut semper placeat spectantibus, orat,   5
>   tentaque ad exemplum sit sua turba dei.

---

adduco (3), **adduxi, adductus**: to contract, tighten
armum, -i *n*: arms, weapons (*pl.*)
circus, -i *m*: a race course
crotalum, -i *n*: castanet
cymbalum, -i *n*: cymbal (*pl.*)
delicia, -ae *f*: a favorite, pet (*pl.*)
doctus, -a, -um: learned, skilled
exemplum, -i *n*: example
natis, natis *f*: buttocks (*pl.*), rump
notus, -a, -um: well known

oro (1): to beg, ask for
pello, (3), **pepuli, pulsus**: to beat, strike
placeo (2): to be pleasing to (with *dat.*)
pono (3): to put, place, dedicate
prurigo, pruriginis *f*: lecherous itch
Quintia, -ae *f*: Quintia, a perfomer
specto (1): to observe, watch
tentus, -a, -um: stretched
turba, -ae *f*: crowd
tympanum, -i *n*: small drum (*pl.*)
vibro (1): to brandish, wave

---

magno circo: abl. of place, "very well-known *in the great Circus*"
movere: inf. epexegetic after *docta*, "learned *in moving*"
Priapo: dat. ind. obj., "dedicates *to Priapus*"
adducta manu: abl. of means, "beaten *with her tightened hand*" i.e. her fist
pro quibus: "in exchange for which things" i.e. her instruments
ut ... placeat: pres. subj. in noun clause after *orat*, "prays *that she would be pleasing*"
sit: pres. subj. also after *orat*, "that her crowd *would be* taut"
ad exemplum dei: "taut *in the manner of the god*" i.e. with an erection

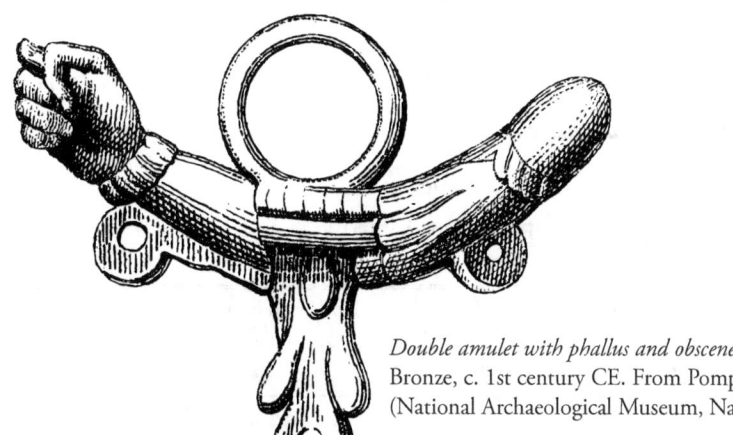

Double amulet with phallus and obscene "fig" gesture. Bronze, c. 1st century CE. From Pompeii. (National Archaeological Museum, Naples.)

XXVIII   HENDECASYLLABLE

Let the thief beware

> Tu, qui non bene cogitas et aegre
> carpendo tibi temperas ab horto,
> pedicabere fascino pedali.
> quod si tam gravis et molesta poena
> non profecerit, altiora tangam.   5

aegre: (*adv.*) scarcely	**pedalis, -e**: measuring a foot
altus, -a, -um: high	**pedico** (1): to sodomize, "assfuck"
carpo (3): to seize. pluck	**poena, -ae** *f*: punishment
cogito (1): to think consider	**proficio** (3), **profeci, profectus**: to make, accomplish, effect
fascinum, -i *n*: an amulet (= *mentula*)	
gravis, -e: heavy painful	**tango** (3): to touch, strike
molestus, -a, -um: annoying	**tempero** (1): to restrain oneself

non bene: litotes, "who understand *not well*"
carpendo: gerundive abl. agreeing with *horto*, "restrain yourself from the garden *worthy of plucking*"
pedicabere: fut. pass. 2 s., "you will be sodomized"
fascino pedali: abl. of means, "with my footlong penis"
quod si: "but if"
si non profecerit: fut. perf. in fut. more vivid protasis, "if such does not accomplish"
tangam: fut. in future more vivid apodosis, "*I will strike* higher (places)" i.e. at the mouth

XXIX   HENDECASYLLABLE

Obscenity is appropriate to Priapus

> Obscenis, peream, Priape, si non
> uti me pudet improbisque verbis.

improbus, -a, -um: shameless	**pudeo** (2): to be ashamed make ashamed
obscenus, -a, -um: obscene	**utor** (3): to make use of (+ *abl.*)
pereo (4), **perii, peritus**: to die, be ruined	

obscenis: abl. pred. with *verbis* below, "use words that are *obscene*"
peream: pres. subj. volitive, "may I die!"
uti: pres. inf. after *pudet*, "if it is not shameful for me *to use*" + abl.

Songs for a Phallic God

sed cum tu posito deus pudore
ostendas mihi coleos patentes,
cum cunno mihi mentula est vocanda.   5

---

coleus, **-i** *m*: sack; (*pl.*) testicles, "balls"   **pateo** (2): to be accessible
cunnus, **-i** *m*: female genitalia (*obsc.*), "cunt"   **pudor, pudoris** *m*: modesty
ostendo (3): to show

---

cum ... ostendas: pres. subj. in circumstantial clause, "when you show"
posito pudore: abl. abs., "with the shame having been set aside"
deus: with concessive force, "although being a god"
mihi: dat. of agent with *vocanda*, "be named *by me*"
est vocanda: pass. periphrastic, "must be named" i.e. the obscene word *mentula* ought to be used with *cunnus*

XXX ELEGAIC COUPLETS

Priapus tells a wayfarer where he can slake his thirst

"Falce minax et parte tua majore, Priape,
    ad fontem, quaeso, dic mihi qua sit iter."
vade per has vites, quarum si carpseris uvam,
    cur aliter sumas, hospes, habebis aquam.

---

aliter: otherwise   **pars, partis** *f*: part
carpo (3), **carpsi**: to seize, pluck   **quaeso** (3): to beg, ask, ask for, seek
falx, falcis *f*: sickle, curved blade   **sumo** (3): to take up, select
fons, fontis *m*: spring, fountain   **uva, -ae** *f*: grape
hospes, hospitis *m*: guest, visitor   **vado** (3): to go, advance
iter, itineris *n*: journey road passage, path   **vitis, -is** *f*: grape vine
minax, minacis (*gen.*): threatening

---

falce ... parte: abl. of means, "threatening *with a sickle ... with your part*"
mihi: ind. obj., "say *to me*"
qua sit: pres. subj. in ind. quest., "tell me *where is* the route"
si carpseris: fut. perf. in future more vivid protasis, "if you will have plucked"
sumas: pres. subj. in parenthetical deliberative question, "why *would you choose* otherwise?"
habebis aquam: a veiled threat of irrumation

XXXI CHOLIAMBS

Let the thief beware

> Donec proterva nil mei manu carpes,
> licebit ipsa sis pudicior Vesta.
> sin, haec mei te ventris arma laxabunt,
> exire ut ipse de tuo queas culo.

---

armum, -i *n*: arms (*pl.*), weapons
carpo (3): to seize, pluck
culus, -i *m*: anus, "asshole"
donec: while, as long as, until
exeo, exire: to exit, pass through
laxo (1): to loosen, open up

protervus, -a, -um: violent
pudicus, -a, -um: chaste, modest
queo (2): to be able
sin: (= **si** + **ne**) but if not
venter, ventris *m*: stomach, womb belly
Vesta, -ae *f*: Vesta, virgin goddess of hearth

---

donec carpes: fut. with conditional force, "*as long as you not pluck* nothing" i.e. if you pluck nothing
proterva manu: abl. of means, "pluck *with a violent hand*"
ipsa Vesta: abl. of comparison, "more chaste *than Vesta herself*"
sis: pres. subj. after *licebit*, "permitted *that you be*"
ut queas: pres. subj. in result clause, "so that you will be able" + inf.
de tuo culo: "through your own ass" because the opening will be so large

XXXII HENDECASYLLABLE

A diatribe against a desiccated hag

> Uvis aridior puella passis,
> buxo pallidior novaque cera,
> collatas sibi quae suisque membris

---

aridus, -a, -um: dry, wrinkled
buxus, -i *f*: boxwood
cera, -ae *f*: beeswax
confero, conferre, contuli, collatus: to compare

membrum, -i *n*: member, limb
novus, -a, -um: new, fresh
pallidus, -a, -um: pale, yellow-green
patior (3), **passus sum**: suffer
uva, -ae *f*: grape

---

uvis: abl. of comparison, "drier *than grapes*"
uvis ... passis: "grapes that have suffered" i.e. raisins
buxo novaque cera: abl. of comparison, "paler *than boxwood and than new beeswax*"
sibi suisque membris: dat. of comparison after *collatas*, "compared *to her and her members*"

Songs for a Phallic God

>formicas facit altiles videri,
>cuius viscera non aperta Tuscus   5
>per pellem poterit videre haruspex,
>quae suco caret ut putrisque pumex,
>nemo viderit hanc ut exspuentem,
>quam pro sanguine pulverem scobemque
>in venis medici putant habere,   10
>ad me nocte solet venire et affert
>pallorem maciemque larualem.
>ductor ferreus insulariaeque
>lanternae videor fricare cornu.

---

affero, afferre: bring to
altilis, -e: fattened, fat
apertus, -a, -um: open, exposed
careo (2): to be without, lack (+ *abl.*)
cornu, cornus *n*: horn, hard covering
ducto (1): to lead
expuo (3): to spit out
ferreus, -a, -um: made of iron
formica, -ae *f*: ant
frico (1): to rub, chafe
haruspex, -icis *m*: soothsayer
insularius, -a, -um: having to do with a neighborhood
lanterna, -ae *f*: lantern
larualis, -e: deathly, ghostly
macies, maciei *f*: leanness

medicus, -i *m*: doctor
nemo, neminis *m*: no one, nobody
pallor, -oris *m*: paleness of complexion
pellis, -is *f*: skin, hide pelt
pulvis, pulveris *m*: powder
pumex, pumicis *m*: pumice stone
putris, -e: rotten, withered
sanguis, sanguinis *m*: blood
scobis, -is *f*: sawdust
soleo (2): to be accustomed to (+ *inf.*)
sucus, -i *m*: juice, moisture
Tuscus, -a, -um: Tuscan, i.e. Etruscan
vena, -ae *f*: blood-vessel
video (2): to see, seem (passive)
viscer, visceris *n*: entrails

---

videri: pres. pass. inf. after *facit*, "causes ants *to seem to be*"
altiles: acc. pred., "seem to be *fat*"
non aperta: concessive, "although not open" i.e. not having been cut open
suco: abl. of seperation after *caret*, "lacks *moisture*"
viderit ut: perf. subj. in result clause, "*so that* no one *has seen*"
quam habere: ind. st. after *putant*, "*whom* the doctors think *to have*"
nocte: abl. of time when, "at night"
ductor … cornu: the reading and interpretation of these last two lines are doubtful. What follows is based on the plausible suggestion of O'Connor.
ductor: pres. pass. ind., "I am introduced (into her)"
ferreus: "(I) *made of iron*" i.e. unfeeling
cornu: acc. obj. of *fricare*, "I seem to scrape *the horn* of a neighborhood lantern"

Priapea

XXXIII

ELEGAIC COUPLETS

A handy girlfriend

Naidas antiqui Dryadasque habuere Priapi,
    et quo tenta dei vena subiret, erat.
nunc adeo nihil est, adeo mea plena libido est,
    ut Nymphas omnis interiisse putem.
turpe quidem factu, sed ne tentigine rumpar,   5
    falce mihi posita fiet amica manus.

---

adeo: to such a degree (that) + *result clause*
amica, -ae *f.*: a girlfriend
antiquus, -a, -um: old
Dryas, Dryados *f.*: a Dryad, a tree nymph
falx, falcis *f.*: a scythe
intereo, interire, interii, interitus: to perish, die
libido, libidinis *f.*: desire
manus, -i, *f.*: hand
Nais, Naidos *f.*: a Naiad, nymph
nympha, -ae *f.*: nymph
plenus, -a, -um: full
pono (3) posui, positus: to place, set aside
quidem: indeed (*postpositive*)
rumpo (3): to break destroy
subeo, subire: to go into
tentigo, tentiginis *f.*: desire
tentus, -a, -um: tight
turpis, -e: ugly, nasty
vena, -ae *f.*: blood-vessel (= *mentula*)

---

habuere: (= *habuerunt*) apocopated perf., "the old Priapuses *possessed*"
quo ... subiret: impf. subj. in rel. clause of characteristic, "*to which* the member *could go*"
erat (sc. **locum**): *locum* is the understood antecedent of *quo*, "*there was a place* to which"
ut putem: pres. subj. in result clause after *adeo*, "such *that I suppose*"
interiisse: perf. inf. in ind. st. after *putem*, "that all the nymphs *have died*"
factu: supine abl. of specification after *turpe*, "terrible thing *to do*"
ne rumpar: pres. subj. in negative purpose clause, "lest I be burst"
tentigine: abl. of means, "lest I be burst *by my desire*"
falce posita: abl. abs., "my scythe having been set aside"
fiet: fut., "my hand *will become*"

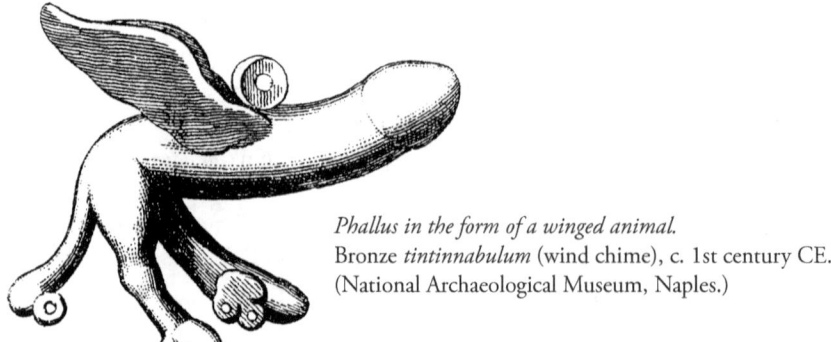

Phallus in the form of a winged animal.
Bronze *tintinnabulum* (wind chime), c. 1st century CE.
(National Archaeological Museum, Naples.)

Songs for a Phallic God

XXXIV   HENDECASYLLABLE

A thank offering to Priapus

> Cum sacrum fieret deo salaci,
> conducta est pretio puella parvo
> communis satis omnibus futura,
> quae quot nocte viros peregit una,
> tot verpas tibi dedicat salignas.   5

---

communis, -e: common
conduco (3), conduxi, conductus: to conduct, introduce
dedico (1): to dedicate
parvus, -a, -um: small, little
perago (3), peregi, peractus: to complete
pretium, pretii *n*: price, value, worth
sacrum, -i *n*: sacrifice
salax, salacis (gen): salacious
salignus, -a, -um: made of willow-wood
satis: enough
unus, -a, -um: alone, a single
verpa, -ae *f*: penis

---

cum fieret: impf. subj. in circumstantial clause, "*when* a sacrifice *was being made*"
deo salaci: dat. of reference, "made *to the salacious god*"
pretio parvo: abl. of value, "a girl *of small value*"
satis: i.e. the price is low enough so that anyone can pay
omnibus: dat. of reference, "for all"
futura: fut. part. expressing purpose, "in order to be"
quot … tot: correlatives, "so many men … so many offerings"
nocte una: abl. of time within which, "in the course of one night"
verpas salignas: i.e. wooden images dedicated to Priapus

XXXV   HENDECASYLLABLE

Let the Thief beware

> Pedicabere, fur, semel, sed idem
> si deprensus eris bis, irrumabo.
> quod si tertia furta molieris,

---

bis: a second time
furtum, -i *n*: theft trick, deception stolen article
idem, eadem, idem: the same
irrumo (1): to orally assault, "facefuck"
molior (3): to undertake, set in motion, plan
pedico (1): to sodomize, "assfuck"
prendo (3), prendi, prensus: to catch, seize
quod si: but if
semel: once
tertius, -a, -um: third

---

pedicabere: fut. pass. 2 s. (= *pedicaberis*), "you will be sodomized"
deprensus eris: fut. perf. pass. in future more vivid protasis, "if *you are seized*"
molieris: fut. in more vivid protasis, "if *you undertake*"

Priapea

ut poenam patiare et hanc et illam,
pedicaberis irrumaberisque. 5

---

patior (3): to suffer, endure   **pedico** (1): to sodomize, "assfuck"

---

ut patiare: pres. subj. in purpose clause, "so that you suffer"
pedicaberis irrumaberisque: fut. perf. pass. in a future more vivid apodosis, "you will be assfucked and facefucked"

XXXVI   CHOLIAMBS

Priapus has his claim to fame too

Notas habemus quisque corporis formas:
Phoebus comosus, Hercules lacertosus,
trahit figuram virginis tener Bacchus,
Minerva flava, lumine est Venus paeto,
frontem vides cornutos Arcades Faunos, 5
habet decentes nuntius deum plantas,
tutela Lemni dispares movet gressus,
intonsa semper Aesculapio barba est,

Arcadis, -e: Arcadian
Bacchus, -i *m*: Bacchus, god of wine
barba, -ae *f*: beard
comosus, -a, -um: having abundant hair
cornutus, -a, um: horned
corpus, corporis *n*: body
decens, decentis (*gen.*): appropriate
dispar, -ris (*gen.*): unequal, disparate, unlike
Faunus, -i *m*: rustic deity of forest
flavus, -a, -um: yellow-haired
forma, -ae *f*: form, figure
frons, frontis *m*: forehead
gressus, -us *m*: steps (*pl.*)
Hercules, Herculis *m*: Hercules (Greek hero of great strength)
intonsus, -a, -um: uncut unshaven
lacertosus, -a, -um: muscular, brawny
lumen, luminis *n*: light, eye (of a person)
Minerva, -ae *f*: Minerva, Roman goddess of wisdom
notus, -a, -um: notable, famous
nuntius, -i *m*: messenger
paetus, -a, -um: squinting slightly
Phoebus, -i *m*: Phoebus Apollo
planta, -ae *f*: heel, foot
tener, -era, -erum: tender
traho (3): to draw, drag, haul derive, get
tutela, -ae *f*: a guardian
virgo, virginis *f*: maiden

---

quisque: nom. subject, "we each one"
lumine paeto: abl. of description, "with squinting eye"
frontem: acc. of respect, "with respect to his forehead"
nuntius deum (=**deorum**): "messenger of the gods" i.e. Mercury
decentes plantas: "appropriate feet" i.e., "winged"
tutela Lemni: i.e. Vulcan, the lame god of the forge located on Lemnos
gressus: acc. cognate, "takes unequal *steps*"
Aesculapio: dat. of possession, "*Aesculapius'* beard is uncut"

nemo est feroci pectorosior Marte:
quod si quis inter haec locus mihi restat, 10
deus Priapo mentulatior non est.

---

ferox, ferocis (*gen.*): wild, bold
locus, -i *m*: rank, position
Mars, Martis *m*: Mars, Roman god of war
mentulatior, -ius: more membered, with a larger *mentula*

nemo, neminis *m*: no one, nobody
pectorus, -a, -um: big-chested
quod si: but if
resto (1): to remain

---

feroci Marte: abl. of comprison, "more big-chested *than ferocious Mars*"
quis (= **aliquis**) **locus**: "if *any position*"
Priapo: abl. of comparison, "more membered *than Priapus*"

XXXVII   HENDECASYLLABLE

Priapus grants a special request from a supplicant

Cur pictum memori sit in tabella
membrum quaeritis, unde procreamur.
cum penis mihi forte laesus esset
chirurgique manum miser timerem,
me dis legitimis nimisque magnis, 5
ut Phoebo puta filioque Phoebi,
curandum dare mentulam verebar.

---

chirurgus, -i *m*: surgeon
curo (1): to cure
filius, -i *m*: son
forte: by chance
laedo (3), **laesi, laesus**: to wound
legitimus, -a, -um: proper
manus, -us *f*: hand
membrum, -i *n*: member, organ
memor, memoris (*gen.*): commemorative

nimis: very much
penis, penis *m*: penis
pingo (3), **pinxi, pictus**: to paint, picture
procreo (1): to procreate, create
puto (1): to suppose
quaero (3): to ask
tabella, -ae *f*: writing tablet
timeo (2): to fear
vereor (2): to fear, dread (+ *inf.*)

---

pictum sit: perf. pass. subj. in ind. question after *quaeritis*, "you ask why *it has been pictured*"
unde procreamur: explaining *membrum*, "whence we are created"
laesus esset: plupf. pass. subj. in *cum* circumstantial cl., "when my penis *was wounded*"
timerem: impf. subj. in cum circumstantial clause, "and when *I was afraid*"
dis legitimis: dat. of agent with *curandum*, "to be cured *by the proper gods*"
ut puta: imperative of *puto* with *ut*, sometimes written as one word, "for example"
filio Phoebi: i.e. Aesculapius, god of medicine
curandum: acc. gerundive after *dare* expressing purpose, "to give my mentula *to be cured*"

Priapea

huic dixi: "fer opem, Priape, parti,
cuius tu, pater, ipse pars videris,
qua salva sine sectione facta   10
ponetur tibi picta, quam levaris,
partem consimilisque concolorque."
promisit fore mentulamque movit
pro nutu deus et rogata fecit.

---

concolor, -oris (*gen.*): of the same color
consimilis, -e: very similar
factum, -i *n*: fact, deed, act achievement
fero, ferre: bring
levo (1): to lift, raise
nutus, -us *m*: nod
ops, opis *f*: help
pars, partis *f*: part, faction
pater, patris *m*: father
pictus, -a, -um: painted
pono (3): to put, set dedicate
promitto (3), **promisi, promissus**: to promise
rogo (1): to ask, ask for
salvus, -a, -um: well
sectio, sectionis *f*: cutting, surgery

---

huic: dat. ind. obj. of *dixi*, "said *to this one*" i.e. to Priapus
parti: ind. obj. of *fer*, "bring *to this part!*" i.e. to the wounded penis
cuius … pars: "whose faction"
videris (sc. **esse**): "you seem (to be)"
qua salva facta: abl. abs., "which thing having been made well"
ponetur: fut. pass., "*will be dedicated* to you"
picta (sc. **mentula**): "a *painted* member"
partem: acc. of respect, "similar in every part"
levaris (= **levaveris**): fut. perf., "which *you will have raised*"
fore (= **futurum esse**): fut. inf. in ind. st., "he promised *that it would be*"
movit: perf., "*he moved* his member"
pro nutu: i.e. instead of nodding his head, as Zeus would do
rogata: neut. pl. acc., "he accomplished *the asked for things*"

XXXVIII   ELEGAIC COUPLETS

Apples for ass

Simpliciter tibi me, quodcunque est, dicere oportet,
  natura est quoniam semper aperta mihi:

---

apertus, -a, -um: open
oportet: it is right
quoniam: because, since
simpliciter: simply

---

me dicere: pres. inf. after *oportet*, "it is right *that I say*"
aperta: pred. adj., "my nature is *open*"

34

pedicare volo, tu vis decerpere poma,
   quod peto, si dederis, quod petis, accipies.

---

accipio (3): to receive
decerpo (3): to pluck, harvest
pedico (1): to sodomize, "assfuck"

peto (3): to desire, ask
pomum, -i *n*: fruit

---

si dederis: fut. perf. in future more vivid protasis, "If you give"

XXXIX

Beauty vs. the Beast

Forma Mercurius potest placere,
forma conspiciendus est Apollo,
formosus quoque pingitur Lyaeus,
formosissimus omnium est Cupido.
me pulchra fateor carere forma,   5
verum mentula luculenta nostra est:
hanc mavult sibi quam deos priores,
si qua est non fatui puella cunni.

Apollo, Apollinis *m*: Apollo
careo (2): to be without, lack (+ *abl.*)
conspicio (3): to see face to face
cunnus, -i *m*: female genitalia (*obsc.*), "cunt"
Cupido, Cupidinis *m*: Cupid
fateor (3): to confess
fatuus, -a, -um: foolish, silly
forma, -ae *f*: form, figure
formosus, -a, -um: beautiful

luculentus, -a, -um: brilliant, splendid
Lyaeus, -i *m*: Lyaeus, Bacchus
malo, malle (3): to prefer
Mercurius, -i *m*: Mercury
pingo (3): to paint, portray
placeo (2): to be pleasing
prior, prioris *m*: prior
pulcher, -a, -um: pretty beautiful

---

forma: abl. of manner, "Mercury is pleasing *in form*"
conspiciendus est: pass. periphrastic, "Apollo *ought to be seen*"
formosus: pred. adj., "Lyaeus is depicted as *beautiful*"
pulchra forma: abl. of separation after *carere*, "that I lack *beautiful form*"
hanc: i.e. mentulam
mavult: 3rd s. pres. of *malo*, "a girl *prefers*"
quam: "*more than* the earlier gods"
si qua (=**aliqua**) **puella**: "any girl"
non fatui cunni: gen. of description, "with a not foolish cunt"

Priapea

XL
ELEGAIC COUPLETS

A prostitute's dedication to Priapus

> Nota Suburanas inter Telethusa puellas,
> > quae, puto, de quaestu libera facta suo est,
> cingit inaurata penem tibi, sancte, corona:
> > hoc pathicae summi numinis instar habent.

---

cingo (3): to surround
corona, -ae *f*: crown, garland
inauro (1): to gild
instar *n* (indeclinable): image, likeness
liber, libera, -um: free
notus, -a, -um: famous
numen, numinis *n*: divine will, divinity
pathicus, -a, -um: sexually perverted
penis, penis *m*: penis
quaestus, -us *m*: gain, profit
Suburanus, -a, -um: having to do with the Suburan quarter in Rome
summus, -a, -um: highest, the top of
Telethusa, -ae *f*: Telethusa cf. 19 above

Suburanas: this quarter in Rome was the red light district
libera: nom. pred., "has made herself *free*"
inaurata ... corona: abl. of means, "surrounded *with a gilded crown*"
sancte: voc. i.e. Priapus
hoc ... instar: "this likeness"
pathicae: nom. pl., "perverted women"

XLI
HENDECASYLLABLE

A curse on erudite poets

> Quisquis venerit huc, poeta fiat
> et versus mihi dedicet jocosos.
> qui non fecerit, inter eruditos
> ficosissimus ambulet poetas.

---

ambulo (1): to walk
dedico (1): to dedicate
eruditus, -a, -um: learned, skilled
ficosus, -a, -um: afflicted with piles
fio (3): to become
jocosus, -a, -um: humorous
poeta, -ae *m*: poet
quisquis, quaeque, quodquod: whoever
versus, -us *m*: verse (of poetry)

venerit: perf. subj. in relative clause of characteristic, "whoever *has come*"
fiat ... dedicet: pres. subj. jussive, "let him become and let him dedicate"
non fecerit: perf. subj. in relative clause of characteristic, "he who *has not made*"
ambulet: pres. subj. jussive, "let him walk"

Songs for a Phallic God

XLII   ELEGIAC COUPLETS

A dedication to Priapus

> Laetus Aristagoras natis bene vilicus uvis
>   de cera facta dat tibi poma, deus.
> at tu sacrati contentus imagine pomi
>   fac veros fructus ille, Priape, ferat.

---

cera, -ae *f*: wax, beeswax
contentus, -a, -um: content with (+ *abl.*)
fructus, -us *m*: fruit
imago, imaginis *f*: likeness, image
laetus, -a, -um: happy
natus, -a, -um: born, produced

pomum, -i *n*: an apple
sacratus, -a, -um: consecrated, dedicated
uva, -ae *f*: grape
verus, -a, -um: true, real
vilicus, -i *m*: farm overseer

---

natis uvis: abl. abs., "with grapes produced by nature"
de cera: wax apples were the offerings to Priapus
deus: voc., "to you, O god" i.e. Priapus
imagine: abl. of specification after *contentus*, "satisfied *with the image*"
ferat: pres. subj. in noun clause after *fac*, "make it *so that he* (Aristagoras) *bears*" i.e. in exchange for the wax offerings

XLIII   ELEGIAC COUPLETS

Pripaus' member is attractive to women

> Velle quid hanc dicas, quamvis sim ligneus, hastam,
>   oscula dat medio si qua puella mihi?
> augure non opus est: "in me" mihi credite, dixit
>   "utetur veris viribus hasta rudis."

---

augur, auguris *m*: diviner, prophet
credo (3): to trust, believe
hasta, -ae *f*: spear
ligneus, -a, -um: wooden
opus, operis *n*: need
osculum, -i *n*: a kiss

quamvis: although (+ *subj.*)
rudis, -e: rough, coarse
utor (3): to make use of (+ *abl.*)
verus, -a, -um: true
vis, vis *f*: strength
volo, velle: to wish, want

---

velle: pres. inf. in ind. question after *dicas*, "say *that* (a girl) *wishes*"
quid dicas: pres. subj. potential, "why would you say?"
quamvis sim: pres. subj. in concessive clause, "*although I am* wooden"
medio: abl. of place where, "in the middle"
si qua puella: "if perchance a girl"
augure: abl. after *opus*, "there is no need for *a diviner*"
dixit: perf., "she said"
veris viribus: abl. of means after *utetur*, "will use its *true strength*"

Priapea

XLIV

Let the thief beware

> Nolite omnia, quae loquor, putare
> per lusum mihi per jocumque dici.
> deprensos ego ter quaterque fures
> omnes, non dubitetis, irrumabo.

---

deprendo (3), **deprendi, deprensus**: to seize, catch
dubito (1): to doubt
fur, -is *m*: a thief
irrumo (1): to orally assault, "facefuck"
jocus, -i *m*: joke

loquor (3): to speak
lusus, -us *m*: play
nolo, nolle: to be unwilling (+ *inf.*)
puto (1): to suppose, think
quater: four times
ter: three times

---

nolite: pres. imper. in prohibition, "Don't!" + inf.
dici: pres. inf. pass. in ind. st. after *putare*, "don't think *that it is said*"
dubitetis: pres. subj. in prohibition where we would expect *ne*, "don't doubt!"

XLV HENDECASYLLABLE

Don't bother curling your hair

> Cum quendam rigidus deus videret
> ferventi caput ustulare ferro,
> ut Maurae similis foret puellae,
> "heus" inquit "tibi dicimus, cinaede,
> uras te licet usque torqueasque,   5

---

cinaedus, -i *m*: catamite, effeminate man
ferrum, -i *n*: an iron tool
fervens, -entis (*gen.*): red hot
licet: although (+ *subj.*)
Maurus, -a, -um: Moorish, North African

rigidus, -a, -um: stiff
similis, -e: like, similar, resembling
torqueo (2): to twist, torture
uro (3): to burn
ustulo (1): to scorch, char

---

videret: impf. subj. in *cum* circumstantial clause, "when *he sees*"
ustulare: inf. in ind. st. after *videret*, "sees some youth *to scorch*"
ferro: abl. means, "scorch *with a curling iron*"
ut foret: impf. subj. in purpose clause, "*in order to be* similar to"
Maurae puellae: dat. after *similis*, "similar *to a Moorish girl*" i.e. to make her hair curly
uras ... torqueasque: pres. subj. concessive after *licet*, "even though *you burn and twist* (your hair)"

num tandem prior es puella, quaeso,
quam sint, mentula quos habet, capilli?"

---

capillus, -i *m*: hair
prior ... quam: more ... than

quaeso (3): to beg, ask, ask for, seek
tandem: finally

---

prior ... quam: "*more* a girl *than* the hairs"
quaeso: parenthetical, "please"
sint: pres. subj. anticipatory after *prior ... quam*, "more than the hairs *would be*"
mentula quos habet: i.e. his pubic hair

XLVI   HENDECASYLLABLE

A diatribe against an old hag

O non candidior puella Mauro,
sed morbosior omnibus cinaedis,
Pygmaeo brevior gruem timenti,
ursis asperior pilosiorque,
Medis laxior Indicisve bracis: 5
mallem scilicet ut libenter ires,
nam quamvis videar satis paratus,

---

asper, -a, -um: rough
braca, -ae *f*: trousers (*pl.*)
brevis, -e: short, little
candidus, -a, -um: bright, white
cinaedus, -i *m*: catamite, effeminate man
gruis, **gruis** *m*: crane
Indicus, -a, -um: Indian
laxus, -a, -um: loose, lax
malo, malle: to prefer
Maurus, -i *m*: Moor (inhabitant of North Africa)

Medus, -a, -um: Median, Persian
morbosus, -a, -um: sickly
paratus, -a, -um: prepared
pilosus, -a, -um: hairy, shaggy
Pygmaeus, -a, -um: of the Pygmies, a legendary African tribe
quamvis: however, although
satis: enough
timeo (2): to fear, be afraid
ursus, -i *m*: bear

Mauro: abl. of comparison, "no whiter *than a Moor*"
omnibus cinaedis: abl. of comparison, "sicker *than all perverts*"
Pygmaeo timenti: abl. of comparison, "shorter *than the Pygmy who fears*" a legendary battle between Pygmies and cranes was a famous subject of art
ursis: abl. of comparison, "rougher *than bears*"
mallem: impf. subj. potential, "I should much prefer"
ut ires: impf. subj. in noun clause after *mallem*, "prefer *that you would go*"
videar: pres. subj. concessive, "although I seem"

> erucarum opus est decem maniplis,
> fossas inguinis ut teram dolemque
> cunni vermiculos scaturrientes.   10

---

dolo (1): to batter, cudgel
eruca, -ae *f*: rocket, an aphrodisiac
fossa, -ae *f*: ditch
inguen, inguinis *n*: groin
maniplus, -i *m*: handful, bundle
opus, operis *n*: need
scaturrio (4): to gush, swarm
tero (3): to rub, wear away
vermiculus, -i *m*: larva, maggot

---

opus est: "there is need for" + abl.
ut teram: pres. subj. in purp. clause, "*in order to rub* the ditches"
ut dolem: pres. subj. in purp. clause, "*in order to batter* the maggots"

XLVII   CHOLIAMBS

A curse on anyone not bringing poetry to dinner

> Quicunque vestrum, qui venitis ad cenam,
> libare nullos sustinet mihi versus,
> illius uxor aut amica rivalem
> lasciviendo languidum, precor, reddat,
> et ipse longa nocte dormiat solus   5
> libidinosis incitatus erucis.

---

amica, -ae *f*: girl friend
cena, -ae *f*: dinner
dormio (4): to sleep
eruca, -ae *f*: rocket, an aphrodisiac
incito (1): to urge, on arouse
languidus, -a, -um: weak, languid
lascivio (4): to act lasciviously
libidinosus, -a, -um: lustful, wanton
libo (1): to pour (a libation) in offering
precor (1): to pray
reddo (3): to return
rivalis, -is *m*: rival (esp. in love)
sustineo (2): to sustain, continue (+ *inf.*)
uxor, -oris *f*: wife
versus, -us *m*: line, verse (of poetry)

---

vestrum: gen. partitive, "whoever *of you*"
libare: pres. inf. complementing *sustinet*, "who continue *to pour out*"
lascivendo: gerund abl. of means, "by acting lasciviously," i.e. by lengthy love-making
languidum: acc. pred., "render his rival *languid*"
reddat: pres. subj. jussive, "*let* his wife *render* his rival"
longa nocte: abl. of time within which, "in a long night"
dormiat: pres. subj. jussive, "let him sleep"
libidinosis erucis: abl. of means, "aroused *by lusty aphrodisiacs*"

XLVIII — HENDECASYLLABLE

Priapus' source of moisture

> Quod partem madidam mei videtis,
> per quam significor Priapus esse,
> non ros est, mihi crede, nec pruina,
> sed quod sponte sua solet remitti,
> cum mens est pathicae memor puellae.   5

---

madidus, -a, -um: wet, moist
memor, -oris (*gen.*): mindful of (+ *gen.*)
mens, mentis *f*: mind
pars, partis *f*: a part, member
pathicus, -a, -um: lascivious, perverse
pruina, -ae *f*: hoar-frost

remitto (3): to send back
ros, roris *m*: dew
significo (1): to signify, indicate, show
soleo (2): to be accustomed to (+ *inf.*)
spons, spontis *f*: free will

---

madidam: acc. pred., "the part that is *wet*"
sponte sua: abl. of manner, "spontaneously"
significor ... esse: the personal form of ind. st., "I am shown to be"
remitti: pres. inf. pass. complementing *solet*, "accustomed *to be returned*" i.e. by an ejaculation

XLIX — ELEGAIC COUPLETS

Don't be offended by these poems

> Tu, quicunque vides circa tectoria nostra
>   non nimium casti carmina plena joci,
> versibus obscenis offendi desine: non est
>   mentula subducti nostra supercilii.

---

castus, -a, -um: pure, moral chaste
desino (3): to stop, cease to (+ *inf.*)
jocus, -i *m*: joke, jest sport
nimium: too much, very
obscenus, -a, -um: obscene
offendo (3): to offend

plenus, -a, -um: full of (+ *gen.*)
subduco (3), **-duxi, -ductus**: to raise up
supercilium, -i *n*: eyebrow, frown, arrogance
tectorium, -i *n*: plastering (of walls)
versus, -us *m*: line, verse (of poetry)

---

non nimium: litotes, "*not too much* chaste" i.e. too little
casti ... joci: gen. after *plena*, "full of not too *chaste jest*"
versibus obscenis: abl. of means, "offended *by obscene verses*"
offendi: pres. pass. inf. in ind. com., "stop *being offended*"
subducti supercilii: gen. of desc., "a prick *with a raised eyebrow*," i.e. a supercilious *mentula*

Priapea

L HENDECASYLLABLE

Priapus' help is sought

Quaedam, si placet hoc tibi, Priape,
ficosissima me puella ludit
et nec dat mihi nec negat daturam,
causas invenit usque differendi.
quae si contigerit fruenda nobis, 5
totam cum paribus, Priape, nostris
cingemus tibi mentulam coronis.

---

causa, -ae *f.*: cause, reason
cingo (3): to surround, encircle
contingo (3) **contigi, contactus**: to reach, attain
corona, -ae *f.*: crown garland
differo, differre: to postpone, delay
ficosus, -a, -um: afflicted with piles
fruor (3): to enjoy (+ *abl.*)
invenio (4): to discover, invent
ludo (3): to mock, tease
nego (1): to deny (+ *inf.*)
par, paris *m*: an equal, partner
placeo (2): to please (+ *dat.*)
totus, -a, -um: whole, all

---

si placet hoc tibi: "if this is pleasing to you," a polite formula
daturam (sc. **esse**): fut. inf. in ind. st. after *negat*, "does not deny *that she will give*"
differendi: gerund gen. after *causas*, "reasons *for delaying*"
si contigerit: fut. perf. in more vivid protasis, "if she will have attained" + part.
fruenda: fut. pass. part. nom. f. supplementing *contigerit*, "attained *enjoying* us," i.e. if she finally enjoys me
cum paribus: "your whole member *with its partners*," i.e. his testicles
nostris … coronis: abl. means, "encircle *with our wreaths*"

LI CHOLIAMBS

Thieves seek not the fruits of Priapus' garden, but the punishment he metes out

Quid hoc negoti est quave suspicer causa
venire in hortum plurimos meum fures,

---

causa, -ae *f.*: cause, reason
negotium, -i *n*: work, business
plurimus, -a, -um: very many
suspicor (1): to mistrust, suspect suppose

---

negoti: gen. of value, "what is this *of business*," i.e. what is the value of this activity?
quave … causa: abl. of cause, "for what reason" i.e. why?
suspicer: pres. subj. in deliberative quest., "why *would I suspect*?"
venire: pres. inf. in ind. st. after *suspicer*, "that many thieves *enter*"

Songs for a Phallic God

cum, quisquis in nos incidit, luat poenas
et usque curvos excavetur ad lumbos?
non ficus hic est praeferenda vicinae   5
uvaeque, quales flava legit Arete,
non mala truncis adserenda Picenis
pirumve, tanto quod periculo captes,
magisque cera luteum nova prunum
sorbumve ventres lubricos moraturum.   10
praesigne rami nec mei ferunt morum

---

adsero (3): to plant near, set near (+ *dat.*)
capto (1): to grasp, seize, reach
cera, -ae *f*: wax, beeswax
curvus, -a, -um: curved, bent
excavo (1): to hollow, scoop out
ficus, -us *f*: fig tree
flavus, -a, -um: golden-haired
incido (3): to fall in with
lubricus, -a, -um: ticklish
lumbus, -i *m*: loins
luo (3): to pay
luteus, -a, -um: yellow
malum, -i *n*: apples
moror (1): to delay
morus, mori *f*: black mulberry
novus, -a, -um: new, extraordinary

periculum, -i *n*: danger, peril
Picenum, -i *n*: Picenum, a region of Italy famous for fruits
pirum, -i *n*: pear
praefero, praeferre: to prefer
praesignis, -e: pre-eminent
prunum, -i *n*: plum
qualis, -e: what kind
quisquis, quaeque, quodquod: whoever
ramus, -i *m*: branch, bough
sorbum, -i *n*: serviceberry
tantus, -a, -um: so much
truncus, -i *m*: trunk (of a tree)
uva, -ae *f*: grape
venter, ventris *m*: stomach
vicinus, -a, -um: neighboring

---

cum…luat…excavetur: pres. subj. in causal clause, "since he pays…and is hollowed out"
usque ad lumbos: "all the way up to the loins," i.e. as deeply as possible
est praeferenda: pass. periphrastic, "ought to be preferred to" + dat.
vicinae (sc. **ficu**): dat. after *praeferenda*, "to my neighbor's (fig)"
uvaeque (sc. **non sunt**): "and there are no grapes here"
quales legit: "of the sort Arete gathers"
Arete: the wife of Alcinous, renowned for his gardens (*Odyssey* 6-8)
non adserenda (sc. **sunt**): pass. periphrastic, "our apples *must not be set near*" + dat., i.e. ought not be compared to
pirumve…prunum…sorbumve: also subjects of *adserenda*
tanto periculo: abl. of circumstance, "with such great danger"
quod captes: pres. subj. in rel. clause of characteristic, "which you would pluck"
cera nova: abl. of specification, "yellow *with newer beeswax*"
moraturum: fut. part., "serviceberry *destined to delay*" i.e. causing constipation

Priapea

nucemve longam, quam vocant Abellanam,
amygdalumve flore purpurae fulgens.
non brassicarum ferre glorior caules
betasve, quantas hortus educet nullus, 15
crescensve semper in suum caput porrum.
nec seminosas ad cucurbitas quemquam
ad ocimumve cucumeresque humi fusos
venire credo sessilesve lactucas
acresque cepas aliumque furatum, 20
nec ut salaces nocte tollat erucas
mentamque olentem cum salubribus rutis.

Abellanus, -a, -um: from Abella
acer, acris, -e: sharp, bitter
alium, -i *n*: garlic
amygdalum, -i *n*: almond
beta, -ae *f*: beet
brassica, -ae *f*: cabbage
caulis, -is *m*: stalk, stem
cepa, -ae *f*: onion
cresco (3): to increase
cucumis, cucumeris *m*: cucumber
cucurbita, -ae *f*: gourd
educo (1): to bring up, produce
eruca, -ae *f*: rocket (an aphrodisiac)
flos, floris *m*: flower, blossom
fulgeo (2): to glow, gleam
fundo (3) **fufi, fusus**: to pour out
furor (1): to steal, plunder
glorior (1): to boast, pride oneself
humus, -i *f*: soil
lactuca, -ae *f*: lettuce
menta, -ae *f*: mint
nux, nucis *f*: nut
ocimum, ocimi *n*: basil
oleo (2): to smell of, smell like
porrum, -i *n*: a leek
purpura, -ae *f*: purple
quantus, -a, -um: how much
ruta, -ae *f*: rue, a bitter herb
salax, -acis (*gen.*): lecherous
saluber, salubris -e: healthy
seminosus, -a, -um: full of seed
sessilis, -e: low-spreading
tollo (3): to remove, steal

Abellanam: a region in the south of Italy known for fruit and nut trees
flore: abl. of manner, "shining *with flower*"
purpurae: gen. of description, "flower *of purple*"
ferre: inf. complementing *glorior*, "I do not boast *to bear*"
quantas ... educet: pres. subj. in ind. question after *glorior*, "*how much* no garden produces"
ad: with acc. expressing purpose, "for my gourds, etc."
quemquam: acc. subject of *venire* below, "nor believe that *anyone* comes"
humi: loc., "poured out *on the ground*"
fusos: perf. part. circumstantial, "cucumbers *that have been poured out*"
furatum: acc. supine expressing purpose after *venire*, "come *to steal*"
ut ... tollat: pres. subj. in purp. clause, "nor *in order to remove*"

quae cuncta quamvis nostro habemus in saepto,
non pauciora proximi ferunt horti.
quibus relictis in mihi laboratum   25
locum venitis, improbissimi fures:
nimirum apertam convolatis ad poenam,
hoc vos et ipsum, quod minamur, invitat.

---

apertus, -a, -um: open
convolo (1): to flock to
cunctus, -a, -um: whole, all
fur, furis *m*: a thief
hortus, -i *m*: garden
improbus, -a, -um: wicked, shameless
invito (1): to invite, attract
laboro (1): to work, be in distress
locus, -i *m*: place
minor (1): to threaten
nimirum: no wonder, no doubt
paucus, -a, -um: small
proximus, -a, -um: very near
quamvis: although
relinquo (3), **reliqui, relictus**: to leave
saeptum, -i *n*: fold, enclosure

---

non pauciora: litotes, "not smaller"
quibus relictis: abl. abs., "which things (i.e. the neighbors' better produce) having been left behind"
laboratum: perf. part. agreeing with *locum*, "a place *that is cared for* by me""

LII   HENDECASYLLABLE

Let the thief beware

Heus tu, non bene qui manum rapacem
mandato mihi contines ab horto,
jam primum stator hic libidinosus
alternis et eundo et exeundo
porta te faciet patentiorem.   5

---

alternis: (adv.) in turn, one after the other
contineo (2): to restrain.
exeo (4): to exit, go out
libidinosus, -a, -um: lustful, wanton
mando (1): to commission, put in charge of
manus, -us *f*: hand
patens, -entis: (*gen.*) open, accessible
porta, -ae *f*: gate
primum: at first, in the first place
rapax, -acis (*gen.*): grasping, rapacious
stator, -oris *m*: one who establishes

---

non bene: understood with *contiens*, "you who *not well* restrain your hand" i.e. who can't stop stealing
mihi: dat. after *mandato*, "garden *commissioned* to me"
stator: a cult title of Jupiter, here Priapus
eundo et exeundo: abl. gerunds, "by entering and exiting"
porta: abl. of comp., "more open *than a gate*"
patentiorem: acc. pred., "will make you *more open*"

Priapea

accedent duo, qui latus tuentur,
pulchre pensilibus peculiati,
qui cum te male foderint jacentem,
ad pratum veniet salax asellus
nilo deterius mutuniatus.   10
quare qui sapiet, malum cavebit,
cum tantum sciat esse mentularum.

---

accedo (3): to come near, approach
asellus, aselli *m*: an ass
caveo (2): to beware
deterius (*adv.*): worse, less
fodio (3), **fodi, fossus** (3): to dig, dig out
jaceo (2): to lie down
latus, lateris *n*: side, flank
male: badly, extremely
malum, mali *n*: harm, malice
mutuniatus, -a, -um: endowed with a *mutunium* (=*mentula*)

peculiatus, -a, -um: endowed
pensilis, -e: hanging, pendant
pratum, -i *n.*: meadow
pulchre: fine, beautifully
quare: wherefore
salax, -acis (gen): lecherous
sapio (3): to understand, have sense
scio (4): to know, understand
tueor (2): to see, look at
tantus, tanta, tantum: so many, so much
venio (4): to come

---

accedunt duo: "two other (punishers) approach"
pensilibus: abl. of specification, "endowed *with hanging* (members)"
foderint: perf. subj. in *cum* circumstantial clause, "when they have dug out"
nilo (= **nihilo**): abl. of difference, "worse *by nothing*"
qui sapiet: fut. in conditional relative clause, "who will be wise" i.e. if he is wise
sciat: pres. subj. in *cum* causal clause, "since he knows"
mentularum: gen. part., "such a large number *of members*"

LIII   ELEGAIC COUPLETS

A supplicant makes a modest dedication to Priapus, but no more modest than what is acceptable to Bacchus and Ceres

Contentus modico Bacchus solet esse racemo,
    cum capiant alti vix cita musta lacus,

---

altus, alta -um: deep
Bacchus, -i *m*: Bacchus, god of wine
capio (3): to hold
citus, cita -um: early
contentus, -a, -um: satisfied, content with (+ *abl.*)

lacus, -us *m*: tank, vat
modicus, -a, -um: modest
mustum, musti *n*: newly fermented wine
racemus, -i *m*: bunch, cluster (of grapes)
soleo (2): to be accustomed to (+ *inf.*)
vix: hardly, scarcely

---

contentus: nom. pred.,"accustomed to be *content with*"
capiant: pres. subj. *cum* concessive clause, "although they scarcely (*vix*) hold" i.e. because there is so much new wine

Songs for a Phallic God

magnaque fecundis cum messibus area desit,
　　in Cereris crines una corona datur.
tu quoque, dive minor, majorum exempla secutus,　　　5
　　quamvis pauca damus, consule poma boni.

---

area, -ae *f*: area, open space
Ceres, Cereris *f*: Ceres, goddess of grain
consulo (3): to consider
corona, -ae *f*: garland, wreath
crinis, -is *m*: hair (*pl.*)
desum, deesse: to be wanting
divus, divi *m*: god
do (1): to give, dedicate
exemplum, -i *n*: example, pattern

fecundus, -a, -um: prolific, abundant
major, -us: greater
messis, messis *m*: harvest, crop
minor, -us: lesser
paucus, -a -um: few (*pl.*)
pomum, -i *n*: fruit
quamvis: although
sequor (3), **secutus sum**: to follow

---

desit: pres. subj. in *cum* concessive clause, "although large enough space *is lacking*" i.e. because the harvests are so abundant
messibus: dat. of reference, "lacking *for harvests*"
dive minor: voc., "Oh minor god" i.e. Priapus
majorum (sc. **deorum**): "the examples *of the greater* gods"
boni: gen. of value with *consule*, "consider them *good*"

LIV   ELEGAIC COUPLETS

An alphabetic threat

"ED" si describas temonemque insuper addas,
　　qui medium vult te scindere, pictus erit.

---

addo (3): add, insert
describo (3): to write down
insuper: in addition
medius, -a, -um: middle

pingo (3), **pinxi, pictus**: to paint, portray
temo, temonis *m*: pole, beam
scindo (3): to cut
velo, velle: to be willing (+ *inf.*)

---

describas...addas: pres. subj. in fut. less vivid protasis, "if *you were to write down... were to add*"
pictus erit: fut. perf. in future more vivid apodosis, whose subject is the antecedent of the relative clause *qui...scindere*, "that which wishes to split you down the middle *will have been portrayed*." The picture will look something like this: E---D which looks something like an erect penis

Priapea

LV   ELEGIAC COUPLETS

Priapus fears losing something worse than his sickle

 Credere quis possit? falcem quoque - turpe fateri -
  de digitis fures subripuere meis.
 nec movet amissi tam me jactura pudorque
  quam praebent justos altera tela metus:
 quae si perdidero, patria mutabor, et olim   5
  ille tuus civis, Lampsace, Gallus ero.

---

amitto (3), **amisi, amissus**: to lose
civis, civis *m*: fellow citizen
credo (3): to trust, believe
digitus, -i *m*: finger
falx, falcis *f*: sickle
fateor (2): to admit, confess
fur, -is *m*: thief
Gallus, -i *m*: Gaul, a priest of Cybele
jactura, -ae *f*: cost
justus, -a -um: just, proper
Lampsacus, -i *m*: Lampascus, the hometown of Priapus
metus, metus *m*: fear

moveo (2): to affect, provoke
muto (1): to move, change
olim: formerly
patria, patriae *f*: native land
perdo (3), **perdidi, perditus**: to lose
praebeo (2): to expose, show
pudor, pudoris *m*: sense of honor
subripio (3), **subripui, subreptus**: to snatch away, steal
tam … quam: so much … as
telum, -i *n*: weapon
turpis, -e: disgraceful, shameful

---

possit: pres. subj. pot., "who could believe?"
fateri: epexegetic inf. after *turpe*, "disgraceful *to confess*"
subripuere: apocopated perf. (=*subripuerunt*), "thieves *have stolen*"
amissi: perf. part. gen. after *jactura*, "nor does the cost *of this thing having been lost* move me"
perdidero: fut. perf. in more vivid protasis, "if *I will have lost* them"
Gallus ero: "I will be a Gaul" but *Gallus* also refers to the castrated priests of Cybelle.

LVI   HENDECASYLLABLE

Priapus is derided by a thief

 Derides quoque, fur, et impudicum
 ostendis digitum mihi minanti?

---

derideo (2): to mock, deride
digitus, -i *m*: finger
fur, furis *m*: thief

impudicus, -a, -um: shameless, unchaste
mino (1): to threaten
ostendo (2): to show, reveal

---

mihi minanti: dat. ind. obj., "show *to me, who is threatening*"

48

eheu me miserum, quod ista lignum est,
quae me terribilem facit videri.
mandabo domino tamen salaci, 5
ut pro me velit irrumare fures.

---

dominus, -i *m*: owner, master
facio (3): to make, cause to be (+ *inf*.)
furs, furis *m*: thief
irrumo (1): to orally assault, "facefuck"
lignum, -i *n*: wood
mando (1): to order

miser, -a -um: miserable
salax, salacis (*gen*.): lecherous, lustful
terribilis, -e: frightful, terrible
video (2): to see, seem (passive)
volo, velle: to wish

---

me miserum: acc. exclamatory, "woe is me!"
ista (sc. **mentula**): nom. subject, "because *this* is wood"
videri: inf. pass. after *facit*, "makes me *seem* terrible"
domino salaci: dat. ind. obj., "command *my lustful master*"
pro me: "on my behald"
ut...velit: pres. subj. in ind. com., "I will order him *to wish*" + inf.

LVII HENDECASYLLABLE

A diatribe against an old woman

Cornix et caries vetusque bustum,
turba putida facta saeculorum,
quae forsan potuisset esse nutrix
Tithoni Priamique Nestorisque,
illis ni pueris anus fuisset, 5

---

anus, anus *f*: old woman, hag
bustum, busti *n*: tomb, corpse
caries, cariei *f*: rottenness
cornix, -icis *f*: a crow
forsan: perhaps
nutrix, nutricis *f*: nurse

possum, posse, potui: to be able
puer, pueri *m*: boy, lad
putidus, -a -um: rotten, decaying
saeculum, -i *n*: age, generation
turba, turbae *f*: commotion, disturbance
vetus, veteris (*gen*.): old, aged

---

turba: abl. of means, "made foul *by the disturbance*" i.e by the effects of aging
putida facta: nom. f. agreeing with the idea of an old woman, not any of the words from the previous sentence describing her, "she, *having been made foul*"
potuisset: plupf. subj. in rel. clause of characteristic, "*who might have been able* to be a nurse"
Tithoni Priamique Nestorisque: gen., all men who reached a legendary old age
illis...pueris: abl. abs., "when they were boys"
ni...fuisset: plupf. subj. in past contrafactual protasis, "if she had not been an old woman" i.e. if she had not been much older even than those men

ne desit sibi, me rogat, fututor.
quid si nunc roget, ut puella fiat? -
"Si nummos tamen haec habet, puella est."

---

desum, deesse: to be wanting
fututor, -oris *m*: a sex partner, "fucker"
nummus, -i *m*: cash, money
puella, -ae *f*: girl
rogo (1): to ask

---

ne desit: pres. subj. in ind. command, "asks that a sex partner *not be lacking from*" + dat.
quid (sc. **dicam**): deliberative question, "what (should I say)?
si roget: pres. subj. in less vivid protasis, "if she should ask"
fiat: pres. subj. in ind. command, "ask *to be come a girl*"
puella est: "she is a girl" i.e. because men will treat her like a girl for money

LVIII   CHOLIAMBS

A curse for thieves

Quicunque nostram fur fefellerit curam,
effeminato verminet procul culo,
quaeque hic proterva carpserit manu poma
puella, nullum reperiat fututorem.

---

carpo (3), **carpsi, carptus**: to seize, pluck
culus, culi *m*: anus, "ass(hole)"
cura, curae *f*: concern, post
effeminatus, -a, -um: womanish, effeminate
fallo (3), **fefelli, falsus**: to deceive, cheat
fur, furis *m*: thief
fututor, -oris *m*: a sex partner
procul: away, at distance, far off
manus, -us *f*: hand
pomum, -i *n*: fruit
protervus, -a, -um: violent, impudent
reperio (4): to find, obtain
vermino (1): to have an itch for (+ *dat.*)

---

fefellerit: perf. subj. in relative clause of characteristic, "whatever thief *has cheated*"
curam: i.e. the garden of Priapus
effeminato... culo: dat. after *verminet*, "itch for *an effeminate behind*"
verminet: pres. subj. jussive, "may he itch for" + dat.
proterva... manu: abl. means, "has plucked *with a violent hand*"
carpserit: perf. subj. in relative clause of characteristic, "whatever girl *has plucked*"
reperiat: pres. subj. jussive, "may she never find!"

LIX   HENDECASYLLABLE

Let the thief beware

Praedictum tibi ne negare possis:
si fur veneris, inpudicus exis.

---

exeo, exire: to exit, leave
fur, furis *m*: thief
nego (1): to deny
praedictum, -i *n*: prediction, forewarning
inpudicus, -a, -um: shameless
venio (4), **veni, ventus**: to come

---

ne ... possis: pres. subj. in prohibition, "may you not be able to" + inf.
veneris: fut. perf. in more vivid protasis, "if you come"

LX   ELEGAIC COUPLETS

Si quot habes versus, tot haberes poma, Priape,
   esses antiquo ditior Alcinoo.

---

antiquus, -a -um: old, ancient
ditior -us: richer
pomum, -i *n*: fruit
versus, -us *m*: line, verse (of poetry)

---

quot ... tot: correlatives, "as many ... as"
haberes: impf. subj. in present contrafactual protasis, "if you (now) had"
esses: impf. subj. in present contrafactual apodosis, "you would be"
antiquo Alcinoo: abl. of comparison, "wealthier *than old Alcinous*" whose legendary garden is described in *Odyssey* 6-8.

LXI   HENDECASYLLABLE

The burdens of trees in the garden of Priapus

Quid frustra quereris, colone, mecum,
quod quondam bene fructuosa malus
autumnis sterilis duobus adstem?

---

adsto (1): to stand to
autumnus, -i *m*: autumn, harvest
colonus, -i *m*: farmer
fructuosus, -a -um: fruitful, productive
frustra: in vain
malus, mali *f*: apple tree
queror (3): to complain
quondam: formerly
sterilis, -e: barren, fruitless

---

quod ... adstem: pres. subj in noun clause after *quereris*, complain *that I am still standing*"
fructuosa malus: nom. appositive, "I, once *a productive apple tree*"
autumnis duobus: abl. of time, "sterile *for two autumns*"

Priapea

non me praegravat, ut putas, senectus,
nec sum grandine verberata dura, 5
nec gemmas modo germine exeuntes
seri frigoris ustulavit aura,
nec venti pluviaeve siccitasve,
quod de se quererer, malum dederunt,
non sturnus mihi graculusve raptor 10
aut cornix anus aut aquosus anser
aut corvus nocuit siticulosus:
sed quod carmina pessimi poetae
ramis sustineo laboriosis.

---

anser, anseris *m*: gander
anus, -us, *f.*: an old woman
aquosus, -a -um: living in water
aura, -ae *f*: wind
cornix, -icis *m*: crow
corvus, corvi *m*: raven
durus, -a -um: hard, harsh
exeo, -ire, -ii, -itus: to come forth, emerge
frigus, -oris *n*: cold weather, frost
gemma, -ae *f*: bud
germen, -inis *n*: sprout, shoot
graculus, -i *m*: jackdaw
grando, -inis *f*: hail
laboriosus, -a, -um: laborious, burdened
malum, -i *n*: evil, mischief
modo: just now, recently
noceo (2), nocui, nocitus: to harm (+ *dat.*)

pessimus, -a, -um: worst
pluvia, pluviae *f*: rain, shower
poeta, -ae *m*: poet
praegravo (1): to weigh down, burden
puto (1): to think, suppose
ramus, -i *m*: branch, bough
raptor, raptoris *m*: robber, plunderer
senectus, -tutis *f*: old age
serus, -a -um: late
siccitas, -tatis *f*: drought
siticulosus, -a, -um: thirsty
sturnus, -i *m*: starling
sustineo (2): to support
ustulo (1): to scorch
ventus, -i *m*: wind
verbero (1): to beat, strike

---

grandine dura: abl. of means, "I was not beaten *by hard hail*"
germine: abl. of place from which, "buds coming *from the sprout*"
aura: nom. subject of *ustulavit*, "nor did *a wind* scorch"
de se: referring to the subject of the main clause (the birds of the next lines), not the relative clause, "complain *about them*"
quererer: impf. subj. in relative clause of characteristic, "about which *I would complain*"
malum dederunt: "nor did they (birds) make mischief"
graculusve raptor: hendiadys, "a jackdaw and plunderer" i.e. a plundering jackdaw
cornix anus: hendiadys, "an old woman crow," i.e. an old crow
sed quod: "*but rather* (I am no longer fruitful) *because*"
carmina: these "poems" of the worst poet could be these very poems of Priapus or the dedications to him hung on the tree. The singular *pessimi poetae* favors the first possibility, which would be a humorous comment on Priapus by one of the trees he protects.
ramis... laboriosis: abl. of place, "I sustain *on my burdened limbs*"

LXII   ELEGIAC COUPLETS

Priapus reassures the watch dogs

> Securi dormite, canes: custodiet hortum
> cum sibi dilecta Sirius Erigone.

---

canis, -is *m*: dog
custodio (4): to guard, protect
dilectus, -a -um: beloved, dear
dormio (4): to sleep, rest
Erigone, -es *f*: Erigone, daughter of Icarius
hortus, horti *m*: garden
securus, -a, -um: secure, untroubled
Sirius, Sirii *m*: Sirius, the dog-star and the name of a legendary dog

---

securi: a nominative adjective used adverbially, "sleep *untroubled!*"

cum dilecta… Erigone: abl. of accomp., "with his beloved Erigone" Sirius (or Maera) was a legendary dog who led his mistress Erigone to her father's grave where she committed suicide. Erigone's example of filial piety is a stark contrast to Priapus, but her name may suggest an erection (from *erigo (3), erigi, erectus*)

LXIII   CHOLIAMBS

Priapus complains

> Parum est, quod hic cum fixerunt mihi sedem,
> agente terra per caniculam rimas
> siticulosam sustinemus aestatem?
> parum, quod hiemis perfluunt sinus imbres
> et in capillos grandines cadunt nostros   5
> rigetque dura barba vincta crystallo?

---

aestas, -atis *f*: summer, summer heat
ago (3), **egi, actus**: to do, drive
barba, -ae *f*: beard
cado (3): to fall, sink
canicula, -ae *f*: little dog, Sirius, the dogstar
capillus, -i *m*: hair, hair of head
crystallum, -i *n*: ice
durus, -a -um: hard, rough
figo (3), **fixi, fictus**: to fasten, fix
grando, -inis *f*: hail, hail-storm
hiems, -is *f*: winter
imber, -bris *m*: rain, shower
parum: too, very little
perfluo (3): to flow, run through
rigeo (2): to be stiff or numb
rima, rimae *f*: crack
sedes, sedis *f*: seat, home
sinus, -us *m*: fold (of clothing)
siticulosus, -a, -um: very dry, parched
sustineo (2): to endure
terra, -ae *f*: earth, land
vincio (4), **vinxi, vinctus**: to bind, fetter

---

parum est: "is it too little?" i.e. isn't it enough?

quod … sustinemus: noun clause explaining the main clause, "is it not enough *that we endure*"

cum fixerunt: indicative identifying a precise time, "*when they fixed* this seat for me"

agente terra: abl. abs. "*the earth making* cracks" i.e. from lack of water

per caniculam: temporal, "during the dogstar" i.e. in August when Sirius rises

crystallo: ab. of means, "bound *with ice*"

Priapea

parum, quod acta sub laboribus luce
parem diebus pervigil traho noctem?
huc adde, quod me terribilem fuste
manus sine arte rusticae dolaverunt,   10
interque cunctos ultimum deos numen
cucurbitarum ligneus vocor custos.
accedit istis impudentiae signum,
libidinoso tenta pyramis nervo.
ad hanc puella — paene nomen adjeci —   15
solet venire cum suo fututore,
quae tot figuris, quas Philaenis enarrat,
non inventis, pruriosa discedit.

---

accedo (3): to be added to
addo (3): to add
adjicio (3) **-jeci, -jectus**: to add, increase
ars, artis *f*: skill, craft
cucurbita, -ae *f*: gourd
cunctus, -a, -um: altogether
custos, custodis *m*: guard, sentry
dies, diei *m*: day
discedo (3): to depart, withdraw
dolo (1): to hew
enarro (1): to describe, relate in detail
figura, -ae *f*: shape, figure; sexual position
fustis, -is *m*: staff club, stick
fututor, -oris *m*: a sex partner
impudentia, -ae *f*: shamelessness, effrontery
invenio (4), **inveni, inventus**: to discover
labor, -is *m*: labor, toil, exertion
libidinosus, -a, -um: lustful, wanton
ligneus, -a, -um: wooden
lux, lucis *f*: light, daylight
manus, -us *f*: hand
nervus, -i *m*: sinew, muscle, nerve
nox, noctis *f*: night
numen, -inis *n*: divine will, divinity, god
paene: nearly, almost, mostly
par, paris (*gen*.): equal (to) (+ *dat*.)
pervigil, pervigilis (*gen*.): always watchful
pruriosus, -a, -um: sexually aroused
pyramis, -idis *f*: pyramid (= *mentula*)
rusticus, -a, -um: country, rustic
signum, -i *n*: sign, proof, signal
tendo (3), **tetendi, tentus**: to stretch, distend
terribilis, -e: frightful, terrible
traho (3): to draw, drag
ultimus, -a, um: furthest
voco (1): to call, name

---

quod ... traho: "enough *that I drag?*"
acta ... luce: abl. abs., "*the day having been spent* in labors"
quod ... dolaverunt: "add (the fact) *that they hewed*"
fuste: abl. of specification after *terribilem*, "me, terrible *with a club*"
ultimum ... numen: nom. appositive, "I, *the most remote power*"
ligneus ... custos: nom. pred., "I am called *the wooden guard*"
istis: dat. after *accedit*, "is added *to these*" i.e. what has been listed above
tenta: perf. part. nom., "my pyramid *having been distended*"
ad hanc (sc. **pyramida**): "*to this pyramid she comes*"
paene nomen adjeci: parenthetical, "I almost mentioned her name"
Philaenis: 3rd century BCE author of an illustrated sex manual
figuris ... non inventis: abl. abs., "the positions not having been discovered"

LXIV   HENDECASYLLABLE

Don't give him what he wants

> Quidam mollior anseris medulla
> furatum venit huc amore poenae:
> furetur licet usque, non videbo.

---

anser, anseris *f*: goose	**mollis, -e**: soft, effeminate
furor (1): to steal, plunder	**poena, -ae** *f*: penalty, punishment
licet: although (+ *subj.*)	**usque**: continuously
medulla, -ae *f*: marrow	

---

medulla: abl. of comparison, "softer *than the marrow*"
furatum: acc. supine indicating purpose, "came *in order to steal*"
amore: abl. of cause, "*for the love* of punishment"
furetur: pres. subj. concessive after *licet*, "although he steals"

LXV   ELEGAIC COUPLETS

A prayer to Priapus

> Hic tibi, qui rostro crescentia lilia mersit,
>   caeditur e tepida victima porcus hara:
> ne tamen extraneum facias pecus omne, Priape,
>   horti sit, facias, janua clausa tui.

---

caedo: to cut, slaughter	**lilium, -i** *n*: lily
clausus, -a, -um: closed, inaccessible	**mergo** (3), **mersi, mersus**: to sink, ruin
cresco (3): to thrive, increase	**pecus, pecoris** *n*: herd, flock
extraneus, -a, -um: external	**porcus, -i** *m*: pig, hog
hara, -ae *f*: pen, coop, pigsty	**rostrum, -i** *n*: beak, snout
hortus, -i *m*: garden	**tepidus, -a, -um**: warm, tepid
janua, -ae *f*: door, entrance	**victima, -ae** *f*: victim, animal for sacrifice

---

rostro: abl. of means, "ruined *with his snout*"
victima: nom. in apposition to *porcus*, "the pig is killed *as a victim*"
ne… facias: pres. subj. in negative purpose clause, "lest you make"
extraneum: acc. pred. after *facias*, "make the herd *external*" i.e. lost
sit: pres. subj. jussive, "*let* the door *be* closed"
facias: subj. jussive parenthetical, "may you do it" i.e. please

Priapea

LXVI

HENDECASYLLABLE

She wants what she fears

> Tu, quae ne videas notam virilem
> hinc averteris, ut decet pudicam:
> nimirum, nisi quod times videre,
> intra viscera habere concupiscis.

---

averto (3), **averti, aversus**: to turn away from
concupisco (3): to desire eagerly, long for
decet (2): it is fitting
habeo (2): to have, hold
hinc: from here
nimirum: without doubt
nota, notae *f*: mark, sign
pudicus, -a, -um: chaste, modest
timeo (2): to fear, dread
virilis, -e: manly, virile
viscer, -eris *n*: innermost part of the body

---

ne videas: pres. subj. in negative purpose clause, "lest you see"
notam virilem: = *mentulam*
averteris: perf. subj. in relative clause of characteristic, "you who *have turned away*"
ut decet pudicam: "as befits a chaste girl"
videre: pres. inf. complementing *times*, "what you fear *to see*" i.e. his *mentula*
habere: pres. inf. complementing *concupiscis*, "desire *to have*"

LXVII

ELEGIAC COUPLETS

A word puzzle

> **Pe**nelopes primam **Di**donis prima sequatur
> et primam **Ca**dmi syllaba prima **Re**mi,
> quodque fit ex illis, tu mi deprensus in horto,
> fur, dabis: hac poena culpa luenda tua est.

Cadmus, -i *m*: Cadmus, founder of Thebes
culpa, culpae *f*: crime, injury
deprendo (3), **deprendi, deprensus**: to seize, catch
Dido, Didonis *f*: Dido, queen and founder of Carthage
do (1): to give, pay
fio: (3) to happen, result
fur, furis *m*: thief
hortus, -i *m*: garden
luo (3): to pay, atone
Penelope, -es *f*: Penelope, wife of Odysseus
poena, -ae *f*: punishment
Remus, -i *m*: Remus, brother of Romulus
sequor (3): to follow
syllaba, -ae *f*: syllable

Penelopes: Priapus is spelling out the punishment for thieves from his garden (pe-di-ca-re) by taking the first syllable from each of the names
deprensus: perf. part. with conditional force, "having been (i.e. if you are) caught"
hac... poena: abl. of means, "atoned *with this punishment*"
luenda est: passive periphrastic, "your crime *must be atoned*"

Songs for a Phallic God

LXVIII
ELEGAIC COUPLETS

A Priapus does some Homeric literary criticism

Rusticus indocte si quid dixisse videbor,
    da veniam: libros non lego, poma lego.
sed rudis hic dominum totiens audire legentem
    cogor Homereas edidicique notas.
ille vocat, quod nos "psolen," ψολόεντα κεραυνόν,   5
    et quod nos culum, κουλεόν ille vocat.
μερδαλέον certe si res non munda vocatur,
    et pediconum mentula merdalea est.
quod nisi Taenario placuisset Troica cunno
    mentula, quod caneret, non habuisset opus.   10

---

audio (4): to hear, listen
certe: surely, certainly
cogo (3): to compel
culus, -i *m*: anus, "ass"
cunnus, -i *m*: female genitalia
dominus, -i *m*: lord, master
edisco (3), **edidici**: to learn by heart
Homereus, -a, -um: Homeric
indoctus, -a, -um: untaught, ignorant
lego (3): to read, gather
liber, libri *m*: book
merdaleus, -a, -um: defiled by excrement
mundus, -a -um: clean, pure

nota, -ae *f*: mark, word
opus, operis *n*: need, work
pedico, -onis *m*: one who sodomizes, "assfucker"
placeo (2), **placui, placitus**: to be pleasing to (+ *dat*.)
pomum, -i *n*: apple
psoleos, -i *m*: penis
rudis, -e: rough, wild, coarse
rusticus, -i *m*: peasant, farmer
Taenarius, -a, -um: Taenarian, Spartan
venia, -ae *f*: favor, pardon
voco (1): to call, name

---

dixisse: perf. inf. after *videbor*, "seem *to have said* anything"
rudis: concessive, "despite being rude"
audire: pres. inf. after *cogor*, "I am compelled *to hear*"
legentem: pres. part. circumstantial, "hear him *reading*"
ψολόεντα κεραυνόν: "smoky thunderbolt," in Homer, with no relationship to ψωλή, a coarse word for a penis
κουλεόν: "sheath (of a sword)" a common metaphor for a vagina
μερδαλέον: *merdaleus* ("filthy") is falsely derived from Homeric σμερδάλεον ("terrible," "awful")
placuisset: plpf. subj. in past contrafactual protasis, "unless *it had been pleasing to*"
Taenario... cunno: dat. after *placuisset,* pleasing *to the Spartan cunt,* i.e. to Helen
Troica... mentula: nom., "the Trojan cock" i.e. Paris
quod caneret: impf. subj. in relative clause of characteristic, "what he (i.e. Homer) would sing"
habuisset: plpf. subj. in past contrafactual apodosis, "*he would have had* no need"

Priapea

mentula Tantalidae bene si non nota fuisset,
  nil, senior Chryses quod quereretur, erat.
haec eadem socium tenera spoliavit amica,
  quaeque erat Aeacidae, maluit esse suam.
ille Pelethroniam cecinit miserabile carmen   15
  ad citharam, cithara tensior ipse sua.
nobilis hinc nata nempe incipit Ilias ira
  principiumque sacri carminis illa fuit.

Aeacides, -ae *m*: descendant of Aeacus, Achilles	**nempe**: truly, certainly, of course
amica, -ae *f*: girl friend	**nobilis, -e**: noble, famous
cano (3), cecini, cantus: to sing, celebrate	**notus., -a, -um**: notorious
carmen, -inis *n*: song, poem	**Pelethronius, -a, -um**: Pelethronian, of the centaur Chiron, the tutor of Achilles
Chryses, -ae *m*: Chryses, father of Chryseis, Agamemnon's prize in *Iliad* 1	**principium, -i** *n*: beginning
	queror (3): to complain, protest
cithara, -ae *f*: cithara, lyre	**sacer, sacra, sacrum**: sacred, holy
Ilias, -adis *f*: the Iliad of Homer	**senior, -oris** *m*: older man
incipio (3): to begin	**socius, -ii** *m*: ally
ira, irae *f*: anger, wrath	**spolio (1)**: to despoil, deprive (+ *abl.*)
malo, malle, malui: to prefer	**tener, -a -um**: delicate, dear
miserabilis, -e: wretched, miserable	**tensus, -a, -um**: stretched, tense
nascor (3), natus sum: to be born	

Tantalidae: gen., "of the descendant of Tantalus" i.e. Agamemnon

fuisset: plpf. subj. in past contrafactual protasis, "if *it had not been* so infamous"

quereretur: impf. subj. in relative clause of characteristic, "nothing which *he would have protested*" i.e. the father of Chryseis would not have complained

erat: the indicative is used in this contrafactual apodosis instead of the subjunctive because the main idea is expressed in the relative clause, "there was nothing (=there would have been nothing) which he would have protested"

haec eadem (sc. **mentula**): nom. subj., "this same (prick)" i.e. Agamemnon

tenera ... amica: abl. of separation, "deprived his ally (Achilles) *of his dear girl*"

esse: pres. inf. after *maluit*, "he preferred (her) *to be*"

suam: acc. pred., "to be *his own*"

ille: i.e. Homer

cithara: abl. of comparison, "tenser than *his cithara*"

ira: abl. of origin, "begins *from anger*" the first word of the *Iliad*

Songs for a Phallic God

altera materia est error fallentis Ulixei,
  si verum quaeras, hunc quoque movit amor.   20
hic legitur radix, de qua flos aureus exit,
  quam cum μῶλυ vocat, mentula μῶλυ fuit.
hic legimus Circen Atlantiademque Calypson
  grandia Dulichii vasa petisse viri.
huius et Alcinoi mirata est filia membrum   25
  frondenti ramo vix potuisse tegi.
ad vetulam tamen ille suam properabat, et omnis
  mens erat in cunno, Penelopea, tuo:

Alcinous, -i *m*: Alcinous, the father of Nausicaa in *Odyssey* 6-8
alter, -a, -um: one (of two), second
amor, amoris *m*: love, sex\
Atlantiadis, -e: of the titan Atlas
aureus, -a, -um: golden
Calypso, -us *f*: Calypso the daughter of Atlas, who detained Odysseus for seven years in *Odyssey* 5
Circe, -es *f*: Circe, the witch of *Odyssey* 9
Dulichius, -a, -um: of Dulichium, an island associated with Odysseus
error, -is *m*: wandering
exeo, -ire, -ii, -itus: to exit, sprout
fallo (3): to deceive
filia, -ae *f*: daughter
flos, floris *m*: flower
frondeo (2): to be leafy
grandis, -e: large, great
lego (3): to read

materia, -ae *f*: material, subject matter
mens, mentis *f*: mind
miror (1), **miratus sum**: to be amazed, look in wonder at
moveo (2), **movi, motus**: to move, provoke
peto (3), **petivi, petitus**: to desire
possum, posse, potui: to be able
propero (1): to hurry
quaero (3): to search for, seek
radix, radicis *f*: root
ramus, -i *m*: branch, bough
tamen: yet, nevertheless, still
tego (3): to cover, hide
Ulixes, Ulixeis *m*: Ulysses, Odysseus, crafty hero of the *Odyssey*
vasum, -i *n*: vessel, equipment (*pl.*)
verum, veri *n*: truth, reality, fact
vetula, -ae *f*: an aging woman
vix: hardly, scarcely

---

illa: *ira* i.e. the wrath of Achilles
legitur: pres. passive, "here a root *is read about*"
μῶλυ: "moly" the magical plant given by Hermes to Odysseus to protect him from the magic of Circe
Circen...Calypson: acc. subj. of *petisse,* "read that *Circe and Calpso desired*"
Dulichii...viri: gen. "the equipment *of the Dulichian man*" i.e. Odysseus
petisse (=*petivisse*): perf. inf. in ind. st. after *legimus*, "we read *that they desired*"
filia: nom., Nausicaa, whom Odysseus approached for help naked except for a branch
ramo: abl. means, "covered *with a branch*"
potuisse: perf. inf. in ind. st. after *mirata est*, "wondered that his member *was scarcely able to*" + inf.
tegi: pres. pass. inf. after *potuisse*, "able *to be covered*"
ad vetulam: i.e. to his wife Penelope

Priapea

quae sic casta manes, ut jam convivia visas
    utque fututorum sit tua plena domus.   30
e quibus ut scires quicunque valentior esset,
    haec es ad arrectos verba locuta procos:
"nemo meo melius nervum tendebat Ulixe,
    sive illi laterum sive erat artis opus.
qui quoniam periit, vos nunc intendite, qualem   35
    esse virum sciero, vir sit ut ille meus."
hac ego, Penelope, potui tibi lege placere,
    illo sed nondum tempore factus eram.

---

arrectus, -a -um: aroused, eager
ars, artis *f*: skill, craft
castus, -a -um: pure, chaste
convivium, -i *n*: banquet, feast
domus, domi *f*: house, home
fututor, -oris *m*: a sexual partner
intendo (3): to exert
latus, lateris *n*: side, flank
lex, legis *f*: principle, condition
loquor (3), locutus sum: to speak
maneo (2): to remain, stay
nemo, neminis *m*: no one, nobody
nervus, -i *m*: sinew, string (of a bow)
nondum: not yet
opus, operis *n*: need, necessity of (+ *gen.*)
pereo (4), perii, peritus: to die
plenus, -a -um: full of (+ *gen.*)
procus, proci *m*: wooer, suitor
qualis, -e: what kind, sort
quoniam: because, since
scio (4): to know, understand
tempus, -oris *n*: time
tendo (3): to stretch, distend
valens, valentis (*gen.*): strong
viso (3): to go to see, look at

---

visas: pres. subj. in result clause, "so chaste *that you go to see*" ironic
sit: pres. subj. in result clause, "so chaste *that your house is full*"
scires: impf. subj. in purpose clause, "in order to know"
esset: impf. subj. in relative clause of characteristic, "know *which is* stronger"
es...locuta: perf. dep., "you spoke"
nervum: In the *Odyssey*, Penelope tests the suitors with a bow contest, which is here transferred humorously to another kind of *nervum*
Ulixe: abl. of comp. after *melius*, "better than my *Odysseus*"
laterum: gen. pl after *opus*, "need *of flanks*" i.e. of his body
intendite: pres. imper., "*exert* yourselves!" but also "make yourselves taut"
qualem esse: pres. inf. in ind. question after *sciero*, "know *what sort of man him to be*"
sciero: fut. perf., "I shall come to know"
sit: pres. subj. in result clause, "so that he *may be*"
hac lege: abl. manner, "by this principle"
potui: perf. past potential, "*I would have been able* to please"
factus eram: plpf., "I had not yet been made"

Songs for a Phallic God

LXIX
HENDECASYLLABLE

Let the thief beware

> Cum fici tibi suavitas subibit
> et jam porrigere huc manum libebit,
> ad me respice, fur, et aestimato,
> quot pondo est tibi mentulam cacandum.

---

aestimo (1): to value, reckon
caco (1): to defecate
ficus, fici *m*: fig
fur, furis *m*: thief
libet (2): it is pleasing, agreeable to (+ *inf.*)
manus, -us *f*: hand
pondo: in or by weight
porrigo (3): to stretch out, extend
quot (*undecl.*): how many
respicio (3): to look back at, consider
suavitas, -tatis *f*: charm, sweetness
subeo, -ire, -ii, -itus: to come up to

tibi: dat. after *subibit,* "approaches *you*"
aestimato: fut. imper. "consider!"
quot pondo est … cacandum: gerundive periphrastic in ind. quest. after *aestimato* "consider *how much in weight must be pooped out*"
mentulam: acc. of respect, "how much weight *in mentula*"

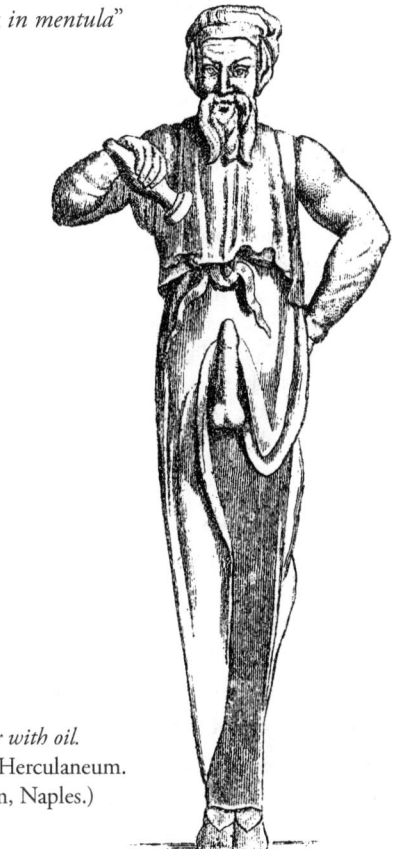

Priapus anointing his erect member with oil.
Bronze, c. 1st century CE. From Herculaneum.
(National Archaeological Museum, Naples.)

Priapea

LXX

HENDECASYLLABLE

Unwanted attention from the neighbor dogs

Illusit mihi pauper inquilinus:
cum libum dederat molaque fusa,
quarum partibus abditis in ignem,
sacro protinus hinc abit peracto.
vicini canis huc subinde venit 5
nidorem, puto, persecuta fumi,
quae libamine mentulae comeso
tota nocte mihi litat rigendo.
at vos amplius hoc loco cavete
quicquam ponere, ne famelicorum 10

---

abdo (3), **abdidi, abditus**: to remove
abeo, abire: to depart, go away
amplus, -a -um: great, large
canis, -is *f*: dog
caveo (2): to beware
comedo (3), **comedi, comesus**: to eat up
famelicus, -a -um: hungry
fumus, -i *m*: smoke
fundo (3), **fudi, fusus**: to pour
ignis, ignis *m*: fire
illudo (3), **illusi, illusus**: to mock, ridicule
inquilinus, -i *m*: tenant, lodger
libamen, -inis *n*: drink-offering, first fruits
libum, -i *n*: cake offering
lito (1): to make offering to (+ *dat.*)
locus, -i *m*: place

mola, -ae *f*: ground meal
nidor, nidoris *m*: strong smell
nox, noctis *f*: night
pars, partis *f*: part, share
pauper, pauperis (*gen.*): poor
perago (3), **peregi, peractus**: to complete
persequor (3), **persecutus sum**: to follow, pursue
pono (3): to put, place
protinus: immediately
puto (1): to suppose
rigeo (2): to be stiff or numb
sacrum, sacri *n*: sacrifice
subinde: immediately after
venio (4), **veni, ventus**: to come
vicinus, -i *m*: neighbor

---

mihi: dat. after *illusit*, "he mocked *me*"
mola fusa: abl. abs., "some meal having been poured out"
partibus abditis: abl. abs., "*parts* of which *went* into the fire" i.e. some accidentally became burnt
sacro ... peracto: abl. abs. "the sacrifice having been completed"
persecuta: perf. part. dep., "she *having followed*"
libamine ... comeso: abl. abs., "the offering having been eaten"
mentulae: gen. of separation, "eaten *off my member*"
tota nocte: abl. time, "throughout the night"
rigendo: gerundive agreeing with *mihi*, "to me *who must be made stiff*"
amplius: acc. adverbial, "anything *more*"
ponere: pres. inf. after *cavete*, "beware *to place* anything"

Songs for a Phallic God

ad me turba velit canum venire,
ne, dum me colitis meumque numen,
custodes habeatis irrumatos.

---

colo (3): to cultivate, worship
custos, custodis *m*: guard, sentry
dum: while, as long as

irrumo (1): to orally assault, "facefuck"
numen, -inis *n*: divine will, divinity
turba, -a *f*: a crowd, pack

---

ne ... velit: pres. subj. in negative purpose clause, "*lest* a pack *wish to*" + inf.
ne ... habeatis: pres. subj. in negative purpose clause, "*lest you have* guards"
irrumatos: perf. part. acc. pred., "have guards that are *facefucked*"

Pan riding an erect mule, with dog and Priapus-herm.
White marble bas-relief, Roman copy of Late Hellenistic original.
(National Archaeological Museum, Naples.)

LXXI   ELEGAIC COUPLETS

Let the thief beware

Si commissa meae carpes pomaria curae,
    dulcia qui doleam perdere, doctus eris.

---

carpo (3): to seize, pluck
committo (3), **-misi, -missus**: to entrust to (+ *dat.*)
cura, -ae *f*: care, responsibility
doceo (2), **docui, doctus**: to teach, show, point out

dulcis, -e: pleasant, sweet
doleo (2): to grieve (+ *inf.*)
perdo (3): to lose
pomarium, -i *n*: orchard

---

si carpes: fut. in future more vivid protasis, "if you pluck"
qui doleam: pres. subj. in relative clause of characteristic, "learned (that I am somone) *who grieves* to lose"
doctus eris: fut. perf. in more vivid apodosis, "you will have learned"

Priapea
LXXII
ELEGAIC COUPLETS

A request and an answer

"Tutelam pomari, diligens Priape, facito:
    rubricato furibus minare mutinio."
Quod moneas non est, quia si furaberis ipse
    grandia mala, tibi, bracchia macra dabo.

---

bracchium, -i *n*: arm, branch
diligens, diligentis (*gen.*): careful, diligent
fur, furis *m*: thief
furor (1): to steal, plunder
grandis, -e: full-grown, large, great
macer, -a -um: thin, meager
minor (1): to threaten (+ *dat*.)
moneo (2): to warn
mutinium, -i *n*: penis
mālum, -i *n*: apple, fruit
mălum, -i *n*: evil, harm
pomarium, -i *n*: orchard
quia: because
rubricatus, -a, -um: painted red
tutela, -ae *f*: tutelage, guardianship

facito: fut. imperative, "may you accomplish!"
rubricato... mutinio: abl. of means, "threaten *with your reddened penis*"
minare: pres. imper. dep., "threaten!"
quod moneas: pres. subj. in relative clause of characteristic, "that *which you warn* is not anything" i.e. is easy to accomplish
si furaberis: fut. in more vivid protasis, "if you yourself steal"
grandia mala: neut. pl. acc., dir. obj. of *furaberis*, "if you steal large fruits"
bracchia macra: neut. pl., "I will give you *empty branches*"; but punning on the Greek words *macra* and *brachys* meaning "long" and "short" in the metrical sense. The Latin word malum with a short "a" means *evil*, with a long "a" means *apple*. Hence the last three words can mean "I will make your longs short" i.e. turn your apples (*māla*) into evils (*măla*).

Phallus in the form of a chimera.
Bronze *tintinnabulum* (wind chime), c. 1st century CE.
(National Archaeological Museum, Naples.)

Songs for a Phallic God

LXXIII   ELEGIAC COUPLETS

An invitation to girls

> Obliquis quid me, pathicae, spectatis ocellis?
>   non stat in inguinibus mentula tenta meis.
> quae tamen exanimis nunc est et inutile lignum,
>   utilis haec, aram si dederitis, erit.

ara, **-ae** *f*: altar, sanctuary	**ocellus**, **ocelli** *m*: (little) eye
do (1), **dedi**, **datus**: to give, dedicate	**pathicus**, **-a -um**: lascivious, perverse
exanimis, **-e**: lifeless, breathless	**specto** (1): to look at
inguen, **-inis** *n*: groin (*pl.*)	**sto** (1): to stand, stand firm
inutilis, **-e**: useless	**tamen**: yet, nevertheless, still
lignum, **-i** *n*: wood, beam	**tentus**, **-a**, **-um**: stretched, distended
obliquus, **-a**, **-um**: slanting, oblique	**utilis**, **-e**: useful

obliquis…ocellis: abl. of manner, "with oblique eyes" i.e. askance
aram: "sanctuary," but also = *cunnum* or *culum*
si dederitis: fut. perf. in more vivid protasis, "if you dedicate"

Brothel scene.
Fresco, c. 50-79 AD. From Pompeii.
(National Archaeological Museum, Naples.)

LXXIV   ELEGIAC COUPLETS

The triple threat of Priapus

> Per medios ibit pueros mediasque puellas
>   mentula, barbatis non nisi summa petet.

barbatus, **-a**, **-um**: bearded	**puella**, **-ae** *f*: girl
medius, **-a**, **-um**: middle of	**puer**, **-i** *m*: boy
nisi: if not, except, unless	**summus**, **-a**, **-um**: highest, the top of
peto, (3): to seek, aim at	

barbatis: dat. of reference, "as for bearded ones"
non nisi: "will *not* go *unless*"
petet: fut. in in more vivid protasis, "unless *it seeks* a higher point" i.e. the mouth

Priapea
LXXV
HENDECASYLLABLE

Priapus has his divine tutelage too

Dodone tibi, Juppiter, sacrata est,
Junoni Samos et Mycena dites,
undae Taenaros aequorumque regi,
Pallas Cecropias tuetur arces,
Delphos Pythius, orbis umbilicum, 5
Creten Delia Cynthiosque colles,
Faunus Maenalon Arcadumque silvas,
tutela Rhodos est beata Solis,

---

aequor, -oris *n*: surface of the sea
Arcadia, ae *f*: Arcadia
arx, arcis *f*: citadel, height
beatus, -a, -um: blessed
Cecropius, -a, um: Cecropian, of Athens
collis, collis *m*: hill
Crete, Cretes *f*: the island of Crete
Cynthius, -a, -um: of Mt. Cynthos
Delia, -ae *f*: the Delian goddess, Diana
Delphi, -orum *m*: Delphi, site of Apollo's most famous oracle
dis, ditis (*gen.*): rich, wealthy
Dodone, -es *f*: Dodona, the oldest Greek oracle
Faunus, -i *m*: deity of forest, herdsman
Juno, Junonis *f*: Juno, wife of Jupiter
Juppiter, Jovis *m*: Jupiter

Maenalos, -i *m*: the Maenalon mountains
Mycena, -ae *f*: Mycene, famous for its wealth
orbis, orbis *m*: circle, world
Pallas, Palladis *f*: Minerva
Pythius, -a, -um: Pythian
rex, regis *m*: king
Rhodos, -i *f*: Rhodes
sacro (1): to make sacred, dedicate
Samos *f*: Samos, Juno's most sacred site
silva, silvae *f*: wood, forest
Sol, Solis *m*: Helius, the sun god
Taeneros, -i *m*: Taenarus, a Greek prominitory
tueor (2): to see, look at, protect
tutela, -ae *f*: guardianship
umbilicus, -i *m*: navel, center
unda, -ae *f*: wave

Dodone: Dodona in NW Greece was sacred to Jupiter
Samos et Mycena: Samos and Mycena were both sacred to Juno
Taenaros: the site of a famous temple to Neptune
regi: dat., "dedicated *to the king* of wave and the seas" i.e. Neptune
Cecropias: Athens is called Cecropian after its legendary king, Cecrops
Pythius: "the Pythian" i.e. Apollo, from the beast (*Pytho*) he slayed at Delphi
orbis umbilicum: the *omphalos* indicating the center of the world was located at Delphi
Creten: Diana was associated with Crete through the Minoan goddess Britomartis
Delia: Apollo and Diana were born on Delos
Cynthios: Mt. Cynthos was on the island of Delos
Maenalon: a mountain range in Arcadia sacred to Pan, with whom Faunus is identified
Rhodos: an island sacred to Helius (Sol) and site of the colossal statue dedicated to him

Songs for a Phallic God

Gades Herculis umidumque Tibur,
Cyllene celeri deo nivosa,   10
tardo gratior aestuosa Lemnos,
Hennaeae Cererem nurus frequentant,
raptam Cyzicos ostreosa divam,
formosam Venerem Gnidos Paphosque
mortales tibi Lampascum dicarunt.   15

---

aestuosus, -a -um: burning hot
celer, -e: swift
Ceres, Cereris *f*: Ceres, goddess of grain
Cyllene, -es *f*: Cyllene, a mountain in central Greece
Cyzicos, -i *f*: Cyzicus, a city in Asia minor
dico (1): to dedicate, consecrate
diva, -ae *f*: goddess
formosus, -a -um: beautiful
frequento (1): to celebrate
Gades, ium *f*: a famous Phoenician site in Spain
Gnidos, -i *f*: Gnidos, a Carian city
gratus, -a -um: pleasing to + dat
Hennaeus, -a, -um: of Henna, the Sicilian city

Hercules, Herculis *m*: Hercules
Lampsacus, -i *f*: Lampsacus, a Greek city on the Troad
Lemnos, -i *f*: the island of Lemnos
nivosus, -a, -um: full of snow
nurus, nurus *f*: daughter-in-law
ostreosus, -a, -um: rich in oysters
Paphos, -i *f*: a city on Cyprus
rapio (3), **rapui, raptus**: to drag off, snatch
tardus, -a -um: slow, limping
Tibur, -uris *n*: Tibur, a Latin city
umidus, -a, -um: damp, moist
Venus, Veneris *f*: Venus, Roman goddess of love and beauty

Gades: site of a temple to Phoenician Melqart, who was conflated with Hercules
Tibur: site of a temple to *Hercules victor*
celeri deo: dat. after *gratior*, "more pleasing *to the swift god*" i.e. to Mercury, who was born on Mt. Cyllene
tardo (sc. **deo**): "to the slow god" i.e. Vulcan, whose forge was on Lemnos
Hennaeae nurus: "the daughters-in-law of Henna" i.e. the women of Henna, the site of a famous old temple to Ceres there.
raptam ... divam: i.e. Persephone, the daughter of Ceres
Cyzicos: Cyzicus was claimed as the site of the rape of Persephone by Pluto, but Henna is the more common one
Gnidos: Gnidos was the site of a famous statue of Venus by Praxiletes
Paphos: Paphos was the birthplace of Venus
tibi: i.e. to Priapus
Lampascum: the hometown of Priapus. cf. 55 above
dicarunt (=*dicaverunt*): syncopated perf., "they have dedicated"

Priapea

LXXVI HENDECASYLLABLE

Priapus' power

> Quod sim jam senior meumque canis
> cum barba caput albicet capillis:
> deprensos ego perforare possum
> Tithonum Priamumque Nestoremque.

---

albico (1): to be white
barba, -ae *f*: beard
canus, -a, -um: white
capillus, -i *m*: hair of head
caput, -itis *n*: head
deprendo (3), **deprendi, deprensus**: to seize, catch
Nestor, -oris *m*: Nestor
perforo (1): to pierce, perforate
Priamus, -i *m*: Priam
senior, -is *m*: an elderly man, senior
Tithonus, -i *m*: Tithonus

---

quod sim ... albicet: pres. subj. in relative clause of characteristic with concessive force, "*although I am* older and my head *is white*"
canis ... capillis: abl. of description, "with white hairs"
deprensos: perf. part. acc. "those caught"
Tithonum: lover of Eos, the dawn, and granted eternal life
Priamum: king of Troy, famously old
Nestorem: the oldest Greek warrior at Troy

LXXVII HENDECASYLLABLE

Don't fence in Priapus!

> Immanem stomachum mihi movetis,
> qui densam facitis subinde saepem
> et fures prohibetis huc adire.
> hoc est laedere, dum juvatis, hoc est
> non admittere ad aucupem volucres. 5

---

adeo, adire: to approach
admitto (3): to permit, admit
auceps, -ipis *m*: bird-catcher
densus, -a -um: thick, dense
fur, furis *m*: thief
immanis, -e: huge, vast
juvo (1): to help, assist
laedo (3): to hurt, injure
moveo (2): to move, stir, agitate
prohibeo (2): to forbid, prevent
saeps, saepis *f*: a hedge, fence
stomachus, -i *m*: stomach, site of anger
volucris, -is *f*: bird

---

stomachum mihi movetis: "you move my stomach" i.e. you move my anger
adire: pres. inf. after *prohibetis*, "prohibit thieves *from coming*"
laedere: pres. inf. nom. predicate, "this is *to harm*"
non admittere: pres. inf. nom. predicate, "this is *not to admit*"

obstructa est via, nec licet jacenti
jactura natis expiare culpam.
ergo qui prius usque et usque et usque
furum scindere podices solebam
per noctes aliquot diesque, cesso.   10
poenas do quoque, quot satis superque est,
in semenque abeo salaxque quondam
nunc vitam perago — quis hoc putaret? —
ut clusus citharoedus abstinentem.

---

abeo, abire: to depart
abstinens, -entis (*gen.*): temperate, chaste
aliquot: some, several
cesso (1): to be inactive, cease from
citharoedus, -i *m*: singer-musician
clusus, -a, -um: closed, locked in
culpa, -ae *f*: fault, blame
dies, diei *m*: day
expio (1): to expiate
jaceo (2): to lie in wait
jactura, -ae *f*: loss, sacrifice
licet (2): it is permitted to (+ *inf.*)
natis, natis *f*: buttocks, rump
nox, noctis *f*: night
nunc: now, today, at present
obstructus, -a, -um: obstructed

perago (3): to carry through to the end
podex, -icis *m*: buttocks, anus
poena, -ae *f*: penalty
prior, prius: earlier, before
puto (1): to believe, suppose
quondam: formerly
salax, salacis (**gen.**): lecherous, lustful
satis: enough, adequate
scindo (3): to tear, rend
semen, -inis *n*: seed
soleo (2): to be in the habit to (+ *inf.*)
super: in addition, besides
usque: all the way
via, viae *f*: way, road
vita, vitae *f*: life

---

jacenti: dat. agreeing with Priapus "nor is it permissible to me *lying in wait*"
jactura: abl. of means "expiate *by means of a sacrifice* of the buttocks"
usque et usque et usque: "further and further up"
poenas do: "I pay penalties"
in semen abeo: "I go to seed" i.e. I expire
vitam … abstinentem: acc. cognate, "I lead *a chaste life*"
quis hoc putaret: impf. subj. in past deliberative question, "who would have imagined this?" i.e. no one would
ut clusus citharoedus: "like a cloistered singer"

at vos, ne peream situ senili,
quaeso, desinite esse diligentes
neve imponite fibulam Priapo.

---

desino (3): to cease (+ *inf.*)	**pereo** (4): to die, perish
diligens, -entis (*gen.*): careful, diligent	**quaeso** (3): to beg, ask
fibula, fibulae *f*: a pin	**senilis, -e**: senile, aged
impono (3): to put X (*acc.*) on Y (*dat.*)	**situs, -us** *m*: situation

ne peream: negative purpose clause "lest I perish"
situ senili: abl. of cause "lest I perish *from a senile situation*"
desinite: imper., "*cease* to be!"
fibulam: a device attached to the penis of a singer to delay puberty (and the consequent voice change)
Priapo: dat. after imponite "don't put a pin *on Priapus*"

LXXVIII   CHOLIAMBS

A curse for a cunnilinguist

At di deaeque dentibus tuis escam
negent, amicae cunnilinge vicinae,
per quem puella fortis ante nec mendax
et quae solebat impigro celer passu
ad nos venire, nunc misella landicae   5
vix posse jurat ambulare prae fossis.

---

ambulo (1): to walk	**juro** (1): to swear
amica, -ae *f*: girl friend	**landica, -ae** *f*: clitoris
ante: before, previously	**mendax, mendacis** (*gen.*): lying, false
celer, -e: swift, quick	**misellus, -a, -um**: poor, wretched
cunnilingus, -i *m*: one who licks the *cunnus*	**nego** (1): to deny
dens, dentis *m*: a tooth	**passus, -us** *m*: step, gait
esca, -ae *f*: food	**prae**: before, because of (+ *abl.*)
fortis, -e: strong, steadfast	**soleo** (2): to be in the habit of
fossa, -ae *f*: ditch	**vicinus, -a, -um**: neighboring
impiger, -gra, -grum: eager, energetic	**vix**: hardly, scarcely

dentibus tuis: dat. of reference, "food *for your teeth*"
negent: pres. subj. jussive, "may the gods deny"
impigro passu: abl of manner, "come *with an eager step*"
posse: pres. inf. in ind. st. after *jurat*, "swears *that she is scarcely able to*" + inf.
prae fossis: "on account of her ditches" i.e. the folds of her vagina, which have become sore

Songs for a Phallic God

LXXIX   CHOLIAMBS

The poet's mighty member

> Priape, quod sis fascino gravis tento,
> quod exprobravit hanc tibi suo versu
> poeta noster, erubescere hoc noli:
> non es poeta fascinosior nostro.

---

erubesco (3): to blush	**gravis**, -e: heavy, painful
exprobro (1): to reproach, upbraid X (*dat.*) about Y (*acc.*)	**nolo, nolle**: to be unwilling
	poeta, -ae *m*: poet
fascinosus, -a, -um: heavily endowed	**tentus**, -a, -um: stretched, extended
fascinum, -i *n*: an amulet (= *mentula*)	**versus, versus** *m*: line, verse (of poetry)

---

quod sis: pres. subj. causal, "*because you are* heavy"
fascino tento: abl. of specification, "heavy *with a tense member*"
quod exprobravit: noun clause in apposition to *hoc* below, "this, namely *that he has reproached*"
hanc (sc. **mentulam**): acc. of respect, "reproached you *for this*"
suo versu: abl. means, "reproached *with his verse*"
hoc: abl. of cause, "blush *because of this*" i.e. the reproach of the poet
noli: imper., "don't!" + inf.
poeta… nostro: abl. of comparison, "more endowed *than our poet*"

LXXX   ELEGAIC COUPLETS

Size doesn't matter

> At non longa bene est, at non bene mentula crassa
>   et quam si tractes, crescere posse putes?
> me miserum, cupidas fallit mensura puellas:

---

crassus, -a -um: thick	**mensura**, -ae *f*: length, size
cresco (3): to increase in size	**miser**, -a -um: miserable, wretched
cupidus, -a -um: eager, passionate	**puella**, -ae *f*: girl
fallo (3): to deceive, disappoint	**puto** (1): to suppose
longus, -a -um: long	**tracto** (1): to handle, manage

---

non longa bene: litotes, "not particularly long"
si tractes: pres. subj. in future less vivid protasis, "which *if you were to handle*"
putes: pres. subj. in future less vivid apodosis, "would you suppose?"
me miserum: acc. exclamation, "O miserable me!"
fallit: "size deceives" i.e. girls suppose that size matters

non habet haec aliud mentula majus ea.
utilior Tydeus qui, si quid credis Homero, 5
ingenio pugnax, corpore parvus erat.
sed potuit damno nobis novitasque pudorque
esse, repellendus saepius iste mihi.
dum vivis, sperare licet: tu, rustice custos,
huc ades et nervis, tente Priape, fave. 10

---

adsum, adesse: be near, be present
corpus, -oris *n*: body
credo (3): to trust, believe
custos, -odis *m*: guard, sentry
damnum, -i *n*: ruin
faveo (2): to favor, support (+ *dat.*)
ingenium, -i *n*: nature, innate quality
licet (2): it is permitted to (+ *inf.*)
major, -us: larger, greater
nervus, -i *m*: muscle, nerve, penis
novitas, -tatis *f*: strangeness, inexperience
parvus, -a -um: small, little

possum, posse, potui: to be able
pudor, -oris *m*: shame
pugnax, -acis (*gen.*): pugnacious
repello: to repel, rebuff
rusticus, -a, -um: homely, rustic
saepius: more often, again and again
spero (1): to hope
tentus, -a, -um: stretched, taut
Tydeus, -i *m*: Diomedes, a Homeric hero
utilis, -e: useful, profitable
vivo (3): to be alive

---

ea: abl. of comp. after *majus*, referring to *mensura*, "this prick has no other thing greater than *that*" i.e. than size

Tydeus: this hero was famous for his ferocity, despite his small stature

Homero: dat. after *credis*, "if one believes *Homer*"

ingenio ... corpore: abl. of specification, "pugnacious *in nature*, although small *in body*"

damno: predicate dat. after *esse*, "could be my *ruin*"

repellendus (sc. **est**): gerundive in periphrastic, "this *must be repelled*" i.e. is a constant obstacle

iste: i.e. pudor

dum vivis: pres. indefinite, "while one is alive"

ades: pres. imper., "be present!"

Glossary

A a

a, **ab**, **abs**: from, by (+ *abl.*)
ad: to, up to, towards (+ *acc.*)
amica, **-ae** *f.*: a girlfriend
aperio, **aperire**, **aperui**, **apertum**: to open
at: but, but yet
aut: or

B b

barba, **-ae** *f.*: a beard
bene: well
bonus, **-a**, **-um**: good, noble

C c

caput, **capitis** *n*: a head
carmen, **-inis** *n*: a song
circa: around, about (+ *acc.*)
coleus, **-i** *m*: sack; (*pl.*) testicles, "balls"
culus, **-i** *m*: anus, "ass(hole)"
cum: with (*prep. + abl.*); when, since, although (*conj. + subj.*)
cunnus, **-i** *m*: female genitalia (*obsc.*), "cunt"
cupido, **-inis** *f.*: desire
cur: why?

D d

de: down from, about, concerning (+ *abl.*)
deus, **-i** *m*; **dea**, **-ae** *f.*: god; goddess
dico, **dicere**, **dixi**, **dictum**: to say, speak
do, **dare**, **dedi**, **datum**: to give
dum: while (+ *indic.*); until (+ *subj.*); provided that (+ *subj.*)
duo: two

E e

ego, **mei**, **mihi**, **me**: I, me
ergo: therefore
et: and

F f

facio, **facere**, **feci**, **factus**: to do, make
fero, **ferre**, **tuli**, **latus**: to bear, carry
forma, **-ae** *f.*: shape, form
fur, **furis** *m*: a thief

H h

habeo, **-ere**, **-ui**, **-itus**: to have, hold
hic, **haec**, **hoc**: this, these
hortus, **-i** *m*: a garden

I i

ille, **illa**, **illud**: that
in: in, on (+ *abl.*); into, onto (+ *acc.*)
inter: between, among; during (+ *acc.*)
intra: within, during (+ *acc.*); (*adv.*) inside
ipse, **ipsa**, **ipsum**: himself, herself, itself
is, **ea**, **id**: he, she, it
iste, **ista**, **istud**: that, that of yours

J j

jam, **jamque**: now; already

L l

licet: it is permitted (+ *inf.*), although (+ *subj.*)

M m

malus, **-a**, **-um**: bad, evil
manus, **-us** *f.*: a hand
membrum, **-e** *n*: body part, member
mentula, **-ae** *f.*: penis (*obsc.*), "dick"
meus, **-a**, **-um**: my, mine

N n

nam: for, indeed, really
ne: lest, that not (+ *subj.*)
nec: and not, nor; **nec...nec**: neither... nor
nemo, neminis: no one
nihil, nil: nothing; not at all
nisi, ni: if not, unless
non: not
nos, nostrum/nostri, nobis, nos: we, us
noster, nostra, nostrum: our
nox, noctis *f*: night
nullus, -a, -um: not any, no one
num: surely not? (*interrogative particle expecting negative answer*)
nunc: now

O o

omnis, -e: all, every, as a whole
opus, operis *n*: work, need

P p

pars, partis *f*: a part
per: through (+ *acc.*)
plenus, -a, -um: full
poena, -ae *f*: punishment
poeta, -ae *m*: poet
pomum, -i *n*: a fruit, apple
possum, posse, potui: to be able, be possible
Priapus, -i *m*: Priapus
primus, -a, -um: first; **primum**: (*adv.*) at first, firstly
pro: for, on behalf of, in proportion to (+ *abl.*)
propter: because of, on account of (+ *acc.*)
puella, -ae *f*: a girl
puto, -are, -avi, -atus: to think, suppose

Q q

quamvis: however, although
qui, quae, quod: who, which, what
quicquam: anything
quicumque, quaecumque, quodcumque: whoever, whatever
quis, quid: who? what? which?
quisquis, quidquid: whoever, whichever
quondam: formerly, once
quoque: also, too
quot: how many?

R r

res, rei *f*: a thing, matter

S s

satis: enough, sufficient
sed: but
semper: always, ever
si: if
sic: in this manner, thus; **sic...ut**: in the same way as
sine: without (+ *abl.*)
soleo, -ere, -ui, -itus: to be accustomed
sub: under, close to (+ *acc.* or *abl.*)
sui, sibi, se/sese: him/her/itself, themselves
sum, esse, fui, futurus: to be, exist
suus, sua, suum: his/her/its (own), (*pl.*) their (own)

T t

tam: so, so much
tamen: nevertheless, still
tendo, tendere, tetendi, tentus: to stretch, extend, direct
teneo, -ere, tenui, tentus: to hold
tot: so many
totus, -a, -um: whole, entire

tu, **tui**, **tibi**, **te**: you (*sing.*)
tuus, **-a**, **-um**: your

U u

unus, **-a**, **-um**: one
usque: up to, continuously
ut, **uti**: as (+ *indic.*); so that, with the result that (+ *subj.*)

V v

venio, **venire**, **veni**, **ventus**: to come
video, **videre**, **vidi**, **visum**: to see, (*pass.*) to seem
vir, **viri** *m*: a man
voco, **-are**, **-avi**, **-atus**: to call, name

NOTES

NOTES

www.ingramcontent.com/pod-product-compliance
Lightning Source LLC
LaVergne TN
LVHW051846080426
835512LV00018B/3091